EGYPT, ISRAEL, SINAI
Archaeological and Historical Relationships
in the Biblical Period

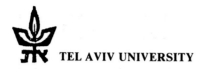 **TEL AVIV UNIVERSITY**

The Kaplan Project on the History of Israel and Egypt:
The Study of the History of Israel and Its Relationship with Egypt
In association with the Kaplan Chair in the History of Egypt and Israel

Other Publications of the Project and the Chair:

Shimon Shamir (ed.)
SELF-VIEWS IN HISTORICAL PERSPECTIVE IN EGYPT AND ISRAEL.
Tel Aviv, 1980.

Joel L. Kraemer (ed.)
PERSPECTIVES ON MAIMONIDES:
PHILOSOPHICAL AND HISTORICAL STUDIES (forthcoming).

Shimon Shamir (ed.)
THE JEWS OF EGYPT: A MEDITERRANEAN SOCIETY
IN MODERN TIMES. Boulder, Co. 1987.

EGYPT, ISRAEL, SINAI

Archaeological and Historical Relationships in the Biblical Period

Edited by

Anson F. Rainey

TEL AVIV UNIVERSITY

Cover Design: Based on a section of a lithograph on the theme of Jewish Egyptian cultural symbiosis in the past. The lithograph was created by Shraga Weil to commemorate the inauguration of the Kaplan Chair in the History of Egypt and Israel.

ISBN: 965-224-008-7

typsetting and printing: Graph-Chen Press Ltd., Jerusalem

Contents

LIST OF PLATES

LIST OF FIGURES AND MAPS

ABBREVIATIONS

ANET — *Ancient Near Eastern Texts*, ed. J.B. Pritchard.
ASAE — *Annales du Service des Antiquités de l'Egypte*
JEA — *Journal of Egyptian Archaeology*
JNES — *Journal of Near Eastern Studies*
V.T. — *Vetus Testamentum*
URK — *Urkunden der 18. Dynastie*, ed. K. Sethe.

Preface

THE studies collected in this book were originally presented at a public symposium, held on April 1st 1982, on Israel, Egypt and Sinai in the Early Biblical Period. The symposium was sponsored jointly by the Project on the History of Israel and Egypt, and the Department of Archaeology and Ancient Near Eastern Cultures at Tel Aviv University. The main theme of the symposium was inspired by the growing public interest in the scientific investigation of the story of the Exodus and its historical background. The subject was originally suggested by Mr. Mendel Kaplan, whose keen interest and devotion for the study of the heritage of the past has facilitated many a project in the field of archaeology. The month of Nissan, the traditional period of the Exodus, was a most appropriate selection for the date of the symposium.

Not all the papers read at the symposium are included here, since for various reasons some of the participants were unavailable or unable to prepare their address in a written form. Most regrettable was our inability to include the study presented by Raphael Giveon, whose sudden passing, in August 1985, was a painful shock to all of us who had shared in this symposium and had been his colleagues for many years. His lecture on the Egyptian Officials Documented in Canaan during the Middle Bronze Age brought to light an important link in the chain of relationships dealt with by the program of the symposium as a whole. Giveon's scholarship is represented in this book by an article on a related subject, compiled from the papers he left behind.

The chapters in this book have been arranged geographically, ranging from Egypt to Canaan. There is one exception to this: The essay by R. Gophna, although it deals with Canaanite sites, was put at the beginning (as it had been at the symposium) because it focuses on an early period, the Early Bronze. The presentations at the evening panel discussion of the Symposium, on the Exodus from an Egyptological point of View, were the basis for the last two chapters. The Keynote address in that panel was delivered by R. Bedford. Of the several responses to his address we bring only that of M. Bietak; other principal participants in the discussion were A. Malat and the late Raphael Giveon.

We wish to thank all those who have helped us in the realization of this project, and particularly Mrs. Edna Liftman of the Dayan Center for Middle Eastern and African Studies who, by dint of her great skill and devotion, has turned a complicated manuscript into an accomplished book. Thanks are also due to Shimon Shamir, the incumbent of the Kaplan Chair in the History of Egypt and Israel, for his encouragement and help throughout the various stages of the project.

At the time of the symposium, there was a flurry of activity on the part of Israeli and other scholars in the wake of the recently signed peace treaty between Israel and Egypt. In many ways, this symposium was an expression of the new expectations which emerged among scholars in this field. It is to be hoped that the appearance of the present publication will contribute to the dialogue between the scholars of the international community and particularly between those of Egypt and Israel. The two countries have a rich and common heritage. We believe it ought to be researched and revealed through true academic co-operation.

A.F. Rainey

1

Egyptian Trading Posts in Southern Canaan at the Dawn of the Archaic Period

Ram Gophna

THE historical analysis of the egyptian finds discovered in Early Bronze Age I-II contexts in Israel during the past thirty years has long been acompanied by reflections regarding the nature of the relations prevailing between Egypt and Canaan during this period (ca. 3200-2650 BCE). The argument focuses around the question: Are these archaeological artifacts merely evidence of reciprocal trade relations between the two countries or do they indicate some kind of Egyptian hegemony over southern Canaan, at least during a part of this period? (for the latest summary of the subject, see Ben-Tor 1982).

Recently the first interpretation has gained favour at the expense of the second (Weinstein 1981; 1984: 69 Ben Tor 1982: 9-11; Beit-Arieh 1984). A survey of the Egyptian finds unearthed

This article follows the chronology for the Predynastic and Archaic periods of W. Kaiser, as set forth by Needler (1984), according to which Narmer was the last king of Dynasty "O" (Late Predynastic period) and Hor-aḥa was the first king of the First Dynasty.

in the EB I-II sites in southern Canaan shows that many of them can be assigned to a relatively short time-span of about 100 years: the end of the Naqada III period (end of the "O" Dynasty) and the reign of the first ruler of the First Dynasty in Egypt, a period that corresponds to the later phase of the Early Bronze Age IB in Canaan (Amiran and Baumgartel 1969:), i.e., ca. 3050-2950 BCE (Needler 1984:27-28, 43). The geographical distribution of the sites in the southern part of the country where these Egyption finds were recovered and an analysis of the functions and character of two of them (see below) show that actually there is no contradiction between the two interpretations, at least not in respect of this particular period.

Following is a list of seven EB IB sites known to us in southern Israel and a description of the Egyptian artifacts found in them that are attributable to the relevant period between late Naqada III and the beginning of the First Dynasty (Fig. 1).

1) *Tel Arad.* In Stratum IV at Tel Arad, which belongs to the Early Bronze Age IB, the Egyptian pottery that was discovered was dated to the reigns of Narmer and Ḥor-aḥa (Amiran 1978:51; 119, n. 67). The most relevant find in this stratum was a storage jar fragment incised with a *serekh* of Narmer (Amiran 1974; 1976).

2) *Small Tel Malḥata.* A considerable quantity of Egyptian pottery was retrieved from the ruins of the EB IB settlement on this tel, which lies some 10 km. southwest of Tel Arad. Among the sherds there were three incised with a *serekh* of Narmer (Amiran a.o. 1983).

3) *'En Besor.* From the analysis of several Egyptian cylinder seal impressions from among the ruins of the Egyptian occupational level (Stratum III), it seems that it was founded at the beginning of the First Dynasty (Gophna 1976a; 1980; Schulman 1980; 1983; Mittmann 1981). A *serekh* of an Egyptian king incised on a potsherd is now also believed to be that of Ḥor-aḥa (Schulman 1976; Kaiser and Dreyer 1982).

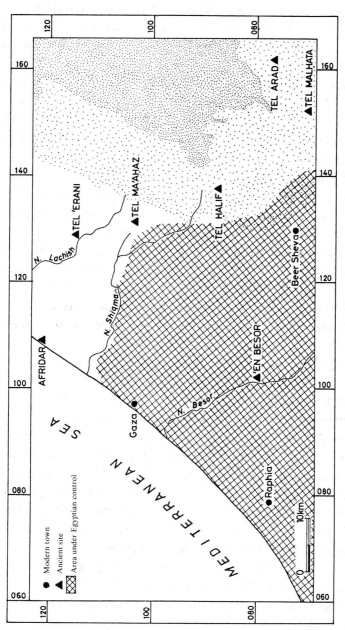

Fig. 1 — The Northwestern Negev in EBA I-II ca 3200-2650 B.C.E

4) *Tel Ḥalif terrace.* Egyptian pottery was first recovered from the surface of the terrace at Tel Ḥalif and later was excavated in the ruins of the EB IB settlement. Among the finds was a storage jar sherd bearing the incised *serekh* of Narmer (Gophna 1972; Amiran a.o. 1983:82).

5) *Tel Ma'aḥaz.* Stratum I of this site yielded an abundance of Egyptian pottery mixed with a small quantity of local wares dating to the Early Bronze Age IB or the beginning of the Early Bronze Age II. Two of the sherds collected from the surface bear traces of *serekh* graffiti. One of these belongs to Dynasty "O", perhaps to Narmer's reign (Gophna 1976b; Amiran 1977; Schulman and Gophna 1981). Accordingly, Stratum I may be dated to the end of the Early Bronze Age IB.

6) *Tel 'Erani.* This site is the first in Israel in which Egyptian artifacts, many of them dating to the late Predynastic period and first Dynasty were found in a clear stratigraphical sequence. A *serekh* of Narmer was incised on a storage jar sherd of Stratum V, which apparently dates to the end of the Early Bronze Age IB (Yeivin 1960; 1961; 1975; Weinstein 1984).

7) *Afridar (Ashkelon).* Several sherds of the late Naqada III period or beginning of the First Dynasty were found in a survey of this EB IB site that lies about 2 km. north-east of Tel Ashkelon (Gophna 1968; 1974: Pls. 15:2-4).

The above seven sites are all located in southern Canaan, one at the southern extremity of the coastal plain ('En Besor), two in the southern coastal plain (Tel 'Erani and Afridar), two in the Beer Sheva-Arad basin (Tel Arad and Small Tel Malḥata) and two in the south-west Judean Shephelah (the Tel Ḥalif terrace and Tel Ma'aḥaz). In five of these sites Egyptian traders apparently lived amongst the Canaanite population, while the other two (Tel Ma'aḥaz and 'En Besor) seem to have been occupied solely by Egyptians (Gophna 1972; 1976b). As may be seen from the distribution map (Fig. 1), the latter two sites lay beyond the borders of permanent Canaanite settlement. The

Egyptian residency at 'En Besor (Stratum III) was built over the ruins of the sole Canaanite settlement (Stratum IV) that existed in the lower Besor basin during the Early Bronze Age IB (Gophna 1976a). The Egyptian outpost at Tel Ma'aḥaz lies about 22 km to its north in the lower basin on Naḥal Shiqma, not far from Canaanite centres such as Tel Ḥasi (Arabic Tell el-Ḥesī; the upper mound; Toombs 1983:33) and Tel 'Erani (Yeivin 1961). Since these two Egyptian settlements were established beyond the border of Canaanite territory, we may assume that the southern coastal plain was a kind of "no-man's land" at the time. Apparently the region was infiltrated not only by the nomads of the Negev Highlands and Sinai but also by Egyptian traders and officials, who were sent by the first Egyptian kings to exploit the situation and to set up trading centers on the doorstep of southern Canaan.

These Egyptian outposts, both of which were built over the ruins of EB I settlements, occupied hilltops close to water sources, one near a well in the wadi bed (Tel Ma'aḥaz) and the second next to a perennial spring ('En Besor). However, they are completely different in respect of their architectural layout and function.

The Tel Ma'aḥaz settlement extended over five dunams at least. Segments of thin walls, floors and various installations, all built of fieldstone, were exposed just under the surface by the excavations. The general impression is of a seasonal camp site of a sparse population that did not remain there long enough to leave any substantial archaeological deposits — except a large quantity of Egyptian pottery, particularly fragments of storage jars of the type used to store and ship various commodities such as oil and grain (Amiran 1977). Judging by the finds, it may be assumed that this was an Egyptian trading post occupied by a band of Egyptian merchants engaged in commerce with the nearby Canaanite settlements. This type of trading post probably enjoyed "free trade" to a greater extent than the Egyptian trading delegations that settled within the Canaanite communities, which were most likely somewhat restricted in their dealings (perhaps subject to taxes?) with the local population (Gophna 1972:52).

At 'En Besor a royal Egyptian trading mission built a large brick structure according to a preconceived plan, possibly of Egyptian derivation. Various Egyptian objects were unearthed in the excavations there, including an abundance of pottery. The springs of 'En Besor, which are the richest in this region and have the most stable flow, could be conveniently guarded and controlled from the hillock on which the residency stood. 'En Besor seems to have served as an official depot, supplying essential provisions (water, bread, and perhaps even beer) to the commercial caravans that travelled to and from Canaan (Gophna and Gazit 1985). Since there were no remnants of storehouses nor an excess of storage jars like those found at Tel Ma'aḥaz, we may assume that 'En Besor's main function was to provide such services rather than to engage in trade. Neither did any jar fragments incised with royal graffiti turn up in the excavations. The explanation for their absence may be connected with the fact that the supplies sent there were mainly for their own consumption or for the passing caravans.

It therefore seems that both outposts were stations in a diversified trade network operating between Egypt and Canaan at this time. They differed from the temporary "overnight" camp sites of the same period that were discovered along the international highway running along the coast of northern Sinai (Oren 1973). This network included stations providing supplies and services (such as 'En Besor), trading posts (such as Tel Ma'aḥaz) and bases for trading delegations that operated inside the Canaanite settlements (for example, Tel 'Erani). This network was active only during the short period that coincided with the socio-economic, political and cultural revolution that took place in Egypt at the end of the Predynastic period and its unification under a single dynasty (Needler 1984:25-31), prior to the urbanization of the Canaanite settlements at Tel Arad and Tel 'Erani (Amiran 1978; Yeivin 1961) and the establishment of a chain of open Canaanite settlements in the Negev Highlands and southern Sinai (Beit-Arieh 1984).

In order to establish and maintain such a trade and service network, Egypt needed to have physical control over the borders of Canaan, and this was feasible only in the southern strip of the coastal plain, where the Egyptians could have a free hand. According to the archaeological evidence, these semi-permanent trading stations were already abandoned at the beginning of the First Dynasty; although commerce between Egypt and Canaan continued to be conducted throughout the rest of this dynasty, the Egyptian presence is absent from the archaeological record of southern Canaan. It may be that the large towns such as Tel 'Erani and Arad, which were on the verge of urbanization at that time, managed to push back the Egyptians from their holdings on the desert border, but it is more likely that we should seek the explanation for the abandonment of these trading posts in the internal developments that occurred in Egypt itself during the First Dynasty (Weinstein 1981).

REFERENCES

Amiran, R., 1974. An Egyptian Jar Fragment with the Name of Narmer from Arad. *IEJ* 24:4-12.

Amiran, R., 1976. The Narmer Jar Fragment from Arad: An Addendum. *IEJ* 26:45-46.

Amiran, R., 1977. Excavations at Tel Ma'aḥaz 1975, 1976. *The Israel Museum News* 12:63-64.

Amiran, R., and Baumgartel, E., 1969. A Second Note on the Synchronism between Arad and the First Dynasty. *BASOR* 195:50-53.

Amiran, R., a.o. 1983. Excavations at Small Tel Malḥata: Three Narmer Sereks. *The Israel Museum Journal* 2:75-83.

Beit-Arieh, I., 1984. New Evidence on the Relations between Canaan and Egypt during the Proto-Dynastic Period. *IEJ* 34:20-23.

Ben-Tor, A., 1982. The Relations between Egypt and the Land of Canaan during the Third Millennium B.C. *Journal of Jewish Studies* 33:3-18.

Gophna, R., 1968. Notes and News: Afridar (Ashkelon). *IEJ* 18:256.

Gophna, R., 1972. Egyptian First Dynasty Pottery from Tel-Ḥalif Terrace. *Museum Haaretz Bulletin* 14:47-52.

Gophna, R., 1974. *The Settlement of the Coastal Plain of Eretz-Israel during the Early Bronze Age* (Ph.D thesis). Tel Aviv University (Hebrew).

Gophna, R., 1976a. Excavations at 'En Besor. *'Atiqot* 11:1-9 (Endish Series).

Gophna, R., 1976b. Egyptian Immigration into Southern Canaan during the First Dynasty. *Tel Aviv* 3:31-37.

Gophna, R., and Gazit, D., 1985. The First Dynasty Egyptian Residency at 'En Besor. *Tel Aviv* 12:9-16.

Kaiser, W., and Dreyer, G., 1982. Umm el-Qaab. Nachuntersuchungen im frühzeitlichen Königsfriedhof 2. Vorbericht. *Mitteilungen des Deutschen Archäologischen Instituts, Abteilung Kairo* 38:211-269.

Mittmann, S.M., 1981. Frühägyptische Siegelinschriften und ein SRH-Emblem des Horus 'Ḥ3 aus dem nördlichen Negeb. *Eretz-Israel* 15:1*-9*. (English section).

Needler, W., 1984. *Predynastic and Archaic Egypt in the Brooklyn Museum.* New York.

Oren, E.D., 1973. The Overland Route between Egypt and Canaan in the Early Bronze Age (Preliminary Report). *IEJ* 23:198-205.

Schulman, A., 1980. More Egyptian Seal Impressions from 'En-Besor. *'Atiqot* 14:17-33. (English series).

Schulman, A., 1983. On the Dating of the Egyptian Seal Impressions from 'En-Besor. *Journal of the Society for the Study of Egyptian Antiquities* 13:249-251.

Schulman, A., and Gophna, R., An Archaic Egyptian *Serekh* from Tel Ma'aḥaz. *IEJ* 31:165-167.

Toombs, L.E., 1983. Tell el-Ḥesī, 1981. *PEQ* 115:25-46.

Yeivin, S., 1960. Early Contact between Canaan and Egypt. *IEJ* 10:193-203.

Yeivin, S., 1961. *First Preliminary Report on the Excavations at Tel "Gat" (Tell Sheykh 'Ahmed el-'Areyny) Seasons 1956-1958.* Jerusalem.

Yeivin, S., 1967. A new Chalcolithic Culture at Tel 'Erani and its Implications for Early Egypto-Canaanite Relations. In: *Fourth World Congress of Jewish Studies: Papers, Vol. 1.* Jerusalem 45-48.

Yeivin, S., 1975. El'Areini, Tell esh Sheikh Ahmed (Tel'Erani). In: Avi-Yonah, M., ed. *Encyclopedia of Archaeological Excavations in the Holy Land I.* Jerusalem:89-97.

Weinstein, J.M., 1981. Egyptian Relations with Palestine in the Early Bronze I-II Period. In: *Annual Meeting of the Society of Biblical Literature, American Academy of Religion: Papers.* San Francisco:1-7.

Weinstein, J.M., 1984. The Significance of Tel'Erani for Egyptian-Palestinian Relations at the Beginning of the Bronze Age. *BASOR* 256:61-69.

2

The Impact of Egypt on Canaan in the Middle Bronze Age

Raphael Giveon

OPPOSITION has been voiced to the theory that there was Egyptian rule in Canaan during Middle Kingdom times. Nonetheless, the existence of such a rule is hinted at in contemporary private inscriptions and literature. Most of the objects dated to the Middle Kingdom found in this country were not in context, and the idea that they came here as a result of grave-robbery and antiquities trade carried out by the Hyksos, does not carry conviction.

Some of the objects can be shown to have come to Canaan during Middle Kingdom times. In our investigations in Sinai we were able to add to the corpus of XII-Dynasty inscriptions found in the turquoise district, including a stela of Sesostris I discovered in Wadi Kharit. The great activity of the Middle Kingdom Pharaohs in Sinai may serve as an indicator of their possible involvement in Canaan.

The untimely death of Professor Raphael Giveon prevented him from presenting his lecture in written form. The ensuing study is a compilation from his previous publications on the subject (Giveon 1976b, 1978, 1980); they represent his views as expressed during the symposium. Editor

I. THE SEALS AS EVIDENCE OF EGYPTIAN RULE IN CANAAN

There exists considerable divergence of opinion on the question
of whether the kings of the XIIth Egyptian Dynasty had a firm
hold over parts of Western Asia, or whether the many Egyptian
objects found in Syria and Palestine came there through trade,
as presents, or with political refugees like Sinuhe. The two
positions may best be summarized by the following quotations:
"In Asia (the XIIth Dynasty) attempted no political empire by
sending out armies to conquer and hold, with resident Egyptian
commissioners in the conquered territory" (Wilson 1951: 134).
— Against: "The Pharaohs of the XIIth Dynasty claimed and
often held the suzerainty over Palestine and Syria, extending
their sphere of influence as far as Ugarit and Qatna... The
imperial organization of the Middle Empire must have been very
loose in comparison with the practice of the New Empire, but the
Palestine of the XIIth Dynasty was poor and thinly populated"
(W.F. Albright 1935: 221).

Besides the statues, sphinxes, jewelry, stone jars, seals of
officials, etc., found in Asia, there is another group of documents
which we propose to discuss here: Seals with names of kings of
the XIIth Dynasty. Scarabs have to be judged according to their
style and, if possible, with reference to the archaeological
context in which they have been found. In Byblos, a jar ("394")
has been found in the "Syrian Temple" (Level IV) which
contained a number of those scarabs and others which were
supposedly of "late type." It has been shown that the jar and its
contents must be dated to Middle Kingdom times at the latest.
This is also proved by analysis of its stratigraphic position: the
jar had been deposited beneath the floor of a Middle Kingdom
Temple and moreover, the temple and its surroundings were not
occupied in Hyksos or Late Bronze times (Negbi and Moskowitz
.1966: 21).

The scarabs bearing names of kings of the XIIth Dynasty, found in Canaan, have to be reconsidered as possible evidence for Middle Kingdom contacts with the Near East.

Not a single seal of Amenemhet I has been found in Canaan. This is in keeping with the rarity of seals of this king in general and with historical events. The greatest number of scarabs discovered in Palestine and Syria and listed below, come from the time of Sesostris I. No. 3 comes from Tomb 24 at Meggido, which was a typical shaft tomb, cut in the time of the XIIth Dynasty and re-used during the Hyksos period. Our scarab may come from the first burial in this tomb, as well as the only scarab which may be assigned (doubtfully) to Amenemhet II (No. 16). The Amethyst scarab from Beth Shean (No. 4) comes from a Late Bronze context. Its material, however, points to a XIIth Dynasty origin. No. 15 comes from a tomb which shows mixed contents of Hyksos and pre-Hyksos implements: this grave is also a shaft tomb, re-used in Hyksos times. There is no reason to doubt that the scarab belongs to the first use of the tomb. From Gezer comes the covering of a jar stopper with four seal impressions of Sesostris I. The fact that a royal seal has been made use of seems to indicate that the jar was stamped in that king's lifetime, on behalf of his administration. Later use of a scarab for sealing is possible, but less probable. From Ugarit comes a carnelian bead, now in the Louvre. From Ugarit also comes, not probably, the seal in the Chabachoff Collection see below). No. 5 and No. 10 come from a Late Bronze context.

There are many scarabs of Sesostris II, mostly of uncertain context. To Hyksos tombs and strata belong No. 19, No. 21, No. 22, No. 24; to the Late Bronze period: No. 26. The Beth Shean scarab (No. 17) comes from a much disturbed level, which belongs to the Middle Kingdom. The Lachish specimen (No. 23) comes from a locus containing Early Bronze together with Hyksos material. No. 27 comes from a shaft tomb containing mixed material, very much like the near-by tomb of the same type in which No. 15 was found.

We have a single scarab, now in the British Museum, with the name of Sesostris III (No. 29); from Tell Jemmeh comes a scarab with the names of Sesostris III and Amenemhet III together (No. 30). It seems unlikely that a later dynasty would have commemorated the co-regency of the two kings.

Amenemhet III is represented by three scarabs: One of uncertain origin (No. 31), the second possibly from the Judean mountains (No. 32), and the third from Tell el-Ajjul (No. 33). There are several cylinder seals from the reign of this king: one from Tell el-Ajjul, one most probably from Ugarit (Chabachoff Collection) and one from Cyprus (Reitler Collection). From Byblos comes a bed bearing the name of the king.

There are, then, a great number of scarabs only from the time of Sesostris I and of Sesostris II; this is in contrast to what we know of the Asiatic preoccupations of Amenemhet II, Sesostris III and Amenemhet III, and to the number of other objects of these kings found in Asia. The fact could be partly explained by a possible change of conditions in the second part of the XIIIth Dynasty, in a way which affected the distribution of scarabs more than other objects. About half of the discoveries mentioned here come from Meggido, Gezer and Tell el-Ajjul. In these three places statues of Egyptian officials of the XIIth Dynasty have been found; the economic and strategic importance of the two first named places for Egypt is amply attested to in documents from the second millennium B.C. Tel el-Ajjul was an important stronghold on what was known at the time of Seti I as the road "from Sileh to Canaan", some 7 kilometers south-west of Gaza. Megiddo, Gezer and Gaza are not mentioned in the execration texts.

The Byblos deposit shows that stylistic features like scrolls, concentric circles or hieroglyphs used as decoration on both sides of the king's name, cannot be taken as evidence of a late,

Hyksos origin of the scarabs. In fact, the number of such scarabs found in a clear Hyksos context is relatively small. It may be that these were manufactured after the time of the XIIth Dynasty, but they may equally be remains of an earlier settlement which have been re-used by Hyksos times or brought up when later inhabitants dug foundation trenches, tombs, etc., in earlier strata.

Other scarabs were found in a Late Bronze stratum; quite a number lack clear context. A group of these scarabs comes from tombs or strata directly related to the time of the XIIth Dynasty. The cylinder seals from Ugarit and Cyprus (see below) are undoubtedly signs of the activity of the Pharaonic administration in these regions.

At least part of the seals with royal names of the XIIth Dynasty can, as we have seen, be considered, together with other documents, as contemporary evidence of Egyptian rule in Canaan.

II.   ROYAL SEALS AND RELATED MATERIAL FROM THE XIIth DYNASTY FOUND IN PALESTINE AND SYRIA

1.   The following abbreviations have been used here:

AG II: W.M.F. Petrie, Ancient Gaza II (London 1932).

AG III: W.M.F. Petrie, Ancient Gaza III (London 1933).

AG IV: W.M.F. Petrie, Ancient Gaza IV (London 1934).

AG V: E.J.H. Mackay and M. Murray, Ancient Gaza V (London 1952). together with W.M.F. Petrie, Cities of the Shepherd Kings.

Gezer II: R.A.S. Macalister, The Excavations of Gezer II, London 1912.

Gezer III: R.A.S. Macalister, The Excavations of Gezer III, London 1912.

Hall, Cat.: H.R. Hall, Catalogue of Egyptian Scarabs etc., in the British Museum, London 1913.

Lachish IV: O. Tufnell, Lachish IV, Oxford 1958.

Megiddo II: G. Loud, Megiddo II, Chicago 1948.

Megiddo Tombs: G. Loud, Megiddo II, Chicago 1948.

Newberry, Scarabs: P.E. Newberry, Scarabs, London 1906.

R.U.A. Rowe, A Catalogue of Egyptian Scarabs... in the Palestine Archaeological Museum, Le Cairo 1936. Scarabs appearing in R. are listed first in each section. Seals which have "Amenemhet" only have been neglected here. Decoration of the scarabs is indicated by "S" for scrolls, "C" for concentric circles, "H" for hieroglyphic signs, mainly decorative, on both sides of the king's name. The others have the name of the king only.

Sesostris I.

1.	YMCA-collection	R.1.
2.		R.2.
3.	Meggido	R.3; Meggido Tombs, Pl, 105, 13 (Tomb 24). H.
4.	Tell el-Ajjul	R.4; AGIV, Pl.4-5, Nr6l. H.
5.	Lachish	R.5; Lachish IV, Pl.39,347. H.
6.	Tell el-Ajjul	R.6; AGII, p.9. Pl.8,145. H.
7.		R.7; AGIV, Pl.6-7,268. S.
8.		R.8; AGIV, Pl.4-5,3. H.
9.	Megiddo	Watzinger, Tell el Mutesellim II (Leipzig 1929), fig. 12,2. S.
10.		Megiddo II, Pl.152, 196.
11.	Gezer	Gezer III, Pl.203, Br. Nrl; Gezer II, p. 315. S.
12.		Gezer III, Pl.205, A Nr9. H.
13.	Gezer	Gezer III, Pl.207,4; Gezer II, p. 319. H.
14.	Beth Shean	A. Rowe, The Topography and History of Beth Shean (Philadelphia, 1930), Pl.34, Nrl. S.
15.	Kafer Garta	Guigues, Bull. Musée de Beyrouth 2, 49, fig. 72. Top row, third from the left. H.

Miscellaneous:

Gezer: Four impressions on sealing covering a jar stopper. Gezer III, Pl.209, 73; p. 330.S.

Ugarit: Bead, carnelian (this is mentioned in: C.F.A. Schaeffer, Ugaritica I (Paris 1939), p. 20, and published in Ugaritica IV, p. 214-5)

Ugarit (most probably): cylinder-seal in the Chabachoff Collection (see below).

Amenemhet II.

16. Megiddo	R.9; Megiddo Tombs, p. 48, Pl.106, 7. H. The attribution to this king is not sure.[2]

Sesostris II.

17. Beth Shean	R.10. H.
18. Tell el-Ajjul	R.11; AGIV, Pl.8-9,365. H.
19. Megiddo	R.12; Megiddo Tombs, Pl.116, 8. H.
20. Tell el-Ajjul	R.13; AGIV, Pl.10-11, 465. H.
21.	AG V, Pl. 9, 1; p. 7. S.
22. Megiddo	Megiddo II, Pl. 150, 109. H.
23. Lachish	Lachish IV, Pl. 30, 31, 63; p. 115. H.
24. Jericho	K. Kenyon, Excavations at Jericho II (London 1965), p. 584, fig. 296, 4. S.
25. Accho (Fig. 34a-c)	Surface find from Tell el-Fukhkhar, the site of ancient Accho. This seal, now at the Municipal Museum, Accho, is 2 cm long, 1.5 cm wide and 0.8 cm high. It is made of white steatite,

the head stylized, elytra not shown;
two notches indicate the division
of the protothorax from the body,
legs are indicated as a double
line. C.

26. 'Amman (Jordan)   W.A. Ward, Cylinders and
                           Scarabs from a Late Bronze
                           Temple at 'Amman. Annual Dep.
                           ant. Jord. 8-9, 52, Pl. 22.
                           H.

27. Kafer Garra   Guiges, Bull. Musée de Beyrouth
                           2, 58, fig. 84 (centre, inverted). H.

28. Shechem   S.H. Horn, JNES 21 (1962) 8, Pl.
                           1, 20; fig. 2, 20. S.

Sesostris III.
29. Gezer   Hall, Cat., p. 302 (Nr 2871).S.

Co-regency of Sesostris III and Amenemhet III.
30. Tell Jemmeh   W.M.F. Petrie, Gerar (London
                           1928), Pl 19,2.

Amenemhet III.
31. YMCA-Collection
    (Jerusalem)
32. Beit Jimal   R., p. 4 (note to No. 14)
33. Tell el-Ajjul   AG II, Pl. 8, 123. H.

Miscellaneous:
Byblos: Bead, white paste. Dunand, Fouilles de Byblos, I, p. 185,
Pl. 127, No. 2905.
Tell el-Ajjul: Cylinder seal (four cylinders united for use as a
bead). R.S.3; AG IV, Pl. 9, No. 352.
Ugarit (most probably): Cylinder seal. Collection Chabachoff
(see below).
Cyprus: Cylinder seal, Reitler Collection (see below).

III. NEW CYLINDER SEALS OF THE XIIth DYNASTY FROM WESTERN ASIA

A.   Sesostris I. Collection B. Chabachoff, Paris

This seal measures 2 cm in height, 0.9 in diameter. It has, like all the cylinders listed here, a small perforation. The object, in excellent condition, is made of light brown jasper, mottled with black. It is inscribed with the prenomen of Sesostris I: Hpr-K3-R'. This seal was bought in Latakia (Syria); it was brought there to a dealer and said to come from near-by Ras Shamra. There is no reason to doubt this, especially in view of other Middle Kingdom finds at Ugarit. Cylinder seals bearing a single cartouche as sole decoration are not uncommon during the XIIth Dyn. The craftsman failed to use the total surface of the seal with the inscription, which is in contradiction to the basic idea of the cylinder seal and shows that he had taken a scarab as a model; it is secondary in its use on a cylinder.

B.   Amenemhet III. Collection B. Chabachoff, Paris

The lower part of this seal is missing. Its actual height is 2.5 cm. The diameter is 0.8 cm. It is made of white paste. The seal was bought in Latakia, as coming from Ras Shamra, together with the above described seal. It is adorned with two vertical cartouches both bearing the prenomen of Amenemhet III, Ny-M't-R'. Above the two cartouches are inscribed epithets of the king, so that the whole reads: Good god, Lord of the Two Lands, Ny-Maat-Re, Son of Re, Ny-Maat-Re.

C.   Amenemhet III. Collection of the late Dr R. Reitler, Haifa

The lower part of this steatite cylinder seal is missing; in its present state it measures 2.7 cm in height by 1 cm in diameter. The object was bought in Cyprus. It has two cartouches inscribed with the prenomen and nomen of Amenemhet III. Above the cartouches there are epithets of the king, so that the whole inscription reads: King of Upper and Lower Egypt, Ny-[Maat]-Re, Good god, Lord of the Two Lands, Amen[emhat]. Before the two cartouches the sign, symbol of stability, has been engraved.

IV. SOME SCARABS FROM CANAAN WITH EGYPTIAN TITLES

We regard Hyksos rule in Canaan as a continuation of the Middle Kingdom rule in the country. The XIIIth Dynasty was an important bridge between XIIth Dynasty influence and the Hyksos. Some royal seals dating to the XIIIth Dynasty have long been known from excavations in this country. To this can now be added yet another group, including a scarab of Hetep-ib-re and another of. Nedjem-ib-re, lesser known kings of the dynasty.

That style of the XIIIth Dynasty scarabs is very similar to the so-called Hyksos-style is not a phenomenon of Palestinian archaeology and not an import into Egypt, but an inner Egyptian development, influenced by foreign ideas. The fact that XIIIth Dynasty scarabs are so very similar to Hyksos scarabs is an additional indication of the continuity of culture and regime (including foreign policy) during the Middle Kingdom and Hyksos periods.

Many of the non-royal seals of the XIIIth Dynasty resemble the well-known Hyksos scarabs so much that, without archaeological context, the two groups can not be distinguished. The close relations between Asia and Egypt at the time of the XIIIth Dynasty are attested to, for example, by the Asiatic slaves of Papyrus Brooklyn published by Hayes; some kings of the dynasty had Semitic names. The seals, new and old, listed here, the relief and the statuette base stress the contact between Western Asia and Egypt at the time. We have no documents of the XIIIth Dynasty speaking of campaigns or victories in Asia. The dynasty was too weak and most of the reigns too short to lay the foundations of an Egyptian presence in Palestine and Syria. For this we have to look to the preceding dynasty. The hold on Asia by the XIIIth Dynasty is the result of the efforts, military, administrative and commercial, of the XIIth Dynasty. The objects of the XIIIth Dynasty found in Asia were similar to those of the XIIth Dynasty and witness a similar manner of Egyptian rule abroad. Byblos and its local rulers already had a special status at the time of Old Kingdom.

The sequence of the 65 rulers of the XIIIth Dynasty shows the lack of stability at home and abroad. No wonder that about half-way through the reign of this Theban Dynasty, northern Egypt and important parts of western Asia fell under Hyksos rule.

All the seals discussed here came from antiquities dealers in Jerusalem or passed through their hands; there is no reason to doubt that their origin is Palestine; however, in most cases the question of their dating remains open, the alternatives being either the Middle Kingdom or the Hyksos period. In either event, the items discussed here are important evidence of the relations between Egypt and Canaan during the Middle Bronze Age; the names and — above all — the titles of the owners of these seals are significant in establishing the extent of Egyptian administration in western Asia during the 12th-16th Dynasties (Rodica Penchas drew the objects and arranged the plates).

Seal 1 (Fig. 1:1) From the collection of M. Dayan. Framed by a thin line, the inscription reads:

śd3wty bity smr w'ty imy-r śd3wt Snb-sw-m-(i)

Treasurer of the King of lower Egypt, the sole friend, Overseer of the Treasury, Snb-sw-m-(i).

The name Snb-sw-m-(i) means, "his health is in my hand" (Ranke 1935:313:21). Martin (1971:117-119) lists some 32 specimens of this name and title: his Nos. 534 and 535 (ibid:46)

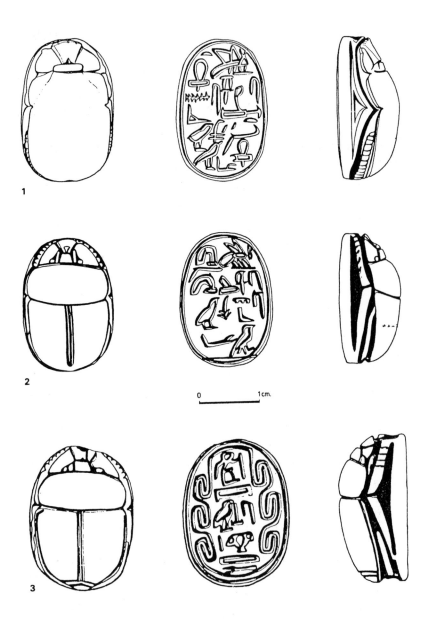

Fig. 1 — 1. Snb-sw-m-(*i*); 2. Snb-sw-m-(*i*); 3. Sḏ3-ḥr.

are orthographic variants of the same name. One scarab from the Brooklyn Museum published by Martin (ibid:118, No. 1528) has been republished recently (James 1974-61, No. 142); so has Martin's No. 1533 (Vodoz 1978:148-149, No. 19886). Several documents show that this important official lived during the 12th Dynasty (Newberry 1906:126). There is no doubt that the scarabs of this particular official should be dated to the Middle Kingdom and not to the Hyksos period.

According to Helck (1958:77-82), the office of "overseer of the treasury" originated in the 11th Dynasty.

Seal 2 (Fig. 1:2). From the collection of R. Braun; framed by a thin line, the inscription reads:

sd3wty bity smr wʻty imy-r sd3wt Snb-sw-m-(i)

Treasurer of the King of Lower Egypt, the sole friend, Overseer of the Treasury, Snb-sw-m-(i).

This scarab, purchased in Jerusalem, was said to have originated in the Hebron region. It has exactly the same titles and names as the previous item, although the titles of Seal 1 are arranged at the lower right and the name appears on the left side in a vertical column, whereas in Seal 2 the titles appear at the top and the name below. Seal 2 has a thin line at the bottom that cuts the frame horizontally on both sides.

Seal 3 (Fig. 1:3). From the collection of R. Braun. Framed by a scroll design, the inscription reads:

smsw hʼyt Sd3-hr m3ʻ hrw

The Elder of the Portal, Sd3-hr, true of voice.

This title is fairly common (Martin 1971:184 [Index]; Gardiner 1947:60-61; Wb II: 476). The personal name occurs in the Middle Kingdom (Ranke 1935:303:6; Martin 1971: 107, Nos. 1376, 1377; No. 1278 is very similar) Martin's example No. 1377 is now published in Hornung and Staehelin (1976:300, No. 549), Martin takes the word as a form of swd3, "to make prosperous", written with the d3 sign only, as in the formula 'nḫ wd3 snb. However, in WbI:399 this form is listed with the notation that it appears almost exclusively in 'nḫ wd3 snb. Besides, the expression would more likely be composed with ·b than with ḥr (Wb I:400, 9 as against Wb IV:378-379 sd3-hr, "to amuse oneself".)

Seal 4 (Fig. 2:1). From the collection of M. Dayan. Framed by a thin line, the inscription reads:

hrp-ḥ S3-rmny
Controller of the Palace, S3-rnmy.

The title occurs on stelas of the Middle Kingdom (Martin 1971:31, No. 331;36, Nos. 396, 401, all of which belong to the same man). The personal name occurs in the Middle Kingdom (Ranke 1935:283:19). Although the first sign of the name looks like 'ayin, it stands for the forearm with palm of hand downwards (Gardiner, sign list D41; see also Wb II:419, 19-20).

Seal 5 (Fig. 2:2). From the collection of R. Braun. Framed by a croll, there is a single column of hieroglyphs reading:

ss n mš' Kmn(i)
The scribe of the army, Kmn(i).

Several instances of this name are known from the Middle Kingdom (Ranke 1935:345:10, Martin 1971: 130, No. 1697). It is of interest to find a seal of an army scribe in Canaan and to ponder as to what kind of military or semi-military mission might have brought him to the country.

Seal 6 (Fig. 2:3). From the R. Braun collection. Framed by a thin line, the inscription reads:

imy-r pr S3-myrt
The Steward S3-mryt.

In the Oriental Institute at Chicago there is a seal with the same title and name, although in this case S3 follows mryt in the

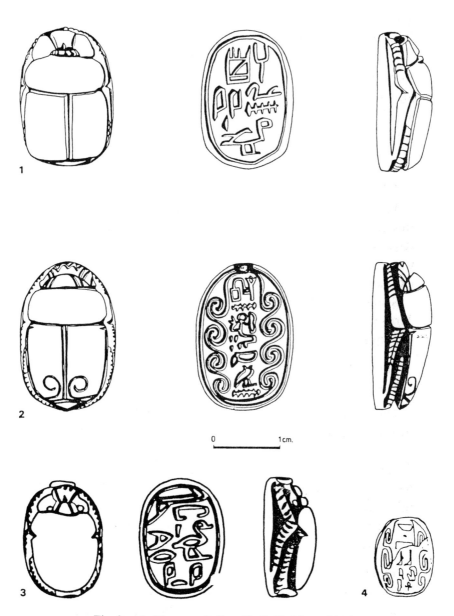

Fig. 2 — 1. S3-rmny; 2. Kmn(*i*); 3. S3-Mryt; 4.Bb*i*.

writing (Martin 1971:101, No. 1299). Since this title is very common, we may have two different people.

Seal 7. This scarab has been seen in the antiquities trade in Jerusalem, but only an impression of the object could be obtained, presented here in photographic reproduction. Within a frame of cord design, there are two vertical columns of hieroglyphs that read:

wr mdw šmʻw S3-mntw
The great one of the Ten of Upper Egypt, S3-mntw

The title is common and two other examples are known from this country, one from ʻAin Samiyah and the other from Acco (Giveon 1974:231); the name, composed with the name of the war god Montlu, occurs frequently in Middle Kingdom sources (Ranke 1935:282:7).

Seal 8 (Fig. 2:4). This has been seen in the antiquities trade in Jerusalem, and although only a drawing could be obtained, we are confident that it is exact. Framed by a scroll

nbt pr Bbi wḥm ʻnḫ
The Lady of the House Bbi, repeating life.

The female name Bbi is popular in the Middle Kingdom (Ranke 1935:95:16), although the only female Bbi in Martin's list is a "servant of the ruler" (Martin 1971:40, No. 447). This is not the only seal of a woman found in this country (Giveon 1976:131, No. 11); it would be interesting to know under what conditions this lady and/or her seal reached the country.

Seal 9 (Fig. 3; Pl. 40:4). From the R. Braun collection. Framed by a scroll design, the inscription reads:

ʻnhn tt ḥq3 Nfr-iw nb im3h
The marine soldier Nfr-iw. lord of honour.

The person's name is well known in the Middle Kingdom (Ranke 1935:194:7; Martin 1971:59, Nos. 704-709). The title has been discussed by Berlev (1971:28, 31, 41). It occurs several times on Middle Kingdom seals (Martin 1971: 12, No. 76, 19, No. 175; 93, No. 1186; 127, No. 1650).

This seal has been listed before, but without illustration (Given 1974:231, No. 6; note 'z' on page 233 with bibliography). It is the only item in this group for which the origin was unequivocally indicated to us by the dealer: 'Ain Samiyah, some 20 kms northwest of Jericho; however, it was not brought to Jerusalem together with the other scarabs and the pottery from the site (Giveon 1974:224-225).

REFERENCES

Albright, W.F., 1935. Presidential Address: Palestine in the Earliest Historical Period. *JPOS* 15:193-234.

Berlev, O.D., 1971. Les pretendus "citadins" au Moyens Empire. *REG* 23:23-48.

Gardiner, A.H., 1947. *Ancient Egyptian Onomastica* I. Oxford.

Gardiner, A.H., 1950. *Egyptian Grammar*. (2nd ed.). London.

Giveon, R., 1974. Hyksos Scarabs with Names of Kings and Officials from Canaan. *Chronique d'Egypte* 49:222-233.

Giveon, R., 1976a. New Egyptian Seals with Titles and Names from Canaan. *Tel Aviv* 3:127-133.

Giveon, R., 1976b. The XII and XIII Dynasties in Canaan and Sinai (MB IIA). Fourth Archaeological Congress in Israel, Jerusalem 17-18 March, 1976. Lecture Summaries: 14.

Giveon R., 1978. *The Impact of Egypt on Canaan*. Göttingen.

Giveon, R., 1980. Some Scarabs from Canaan with Egyptian *Tel Aviv* 7:179-184.

Helck, W., 1958. *Zur Verwaltung des Mittleren und Neuen Reiches*. Leiden.

Hornung, E., and Staehelin, Elisabeth, eds. 1976. *Skarabaen und andere Siegelamulette aus Basler Sammlungen*. Mainz.

James, T.G.H., 1974. *Corpus of Hieroglyphic Inscriptions in the Brooklyn Museum* I. Brooklyn.

Martin, G.T., 1971. *Egyptian Administrative and Private-Name Seals*. Oxford.

Negbi, O., and Moskowitz, S., 1966. The "Foundation Deposits" or "Offering Deposits" of Byblos. *BASOR* 184: 21-26.

Newberry, P.E., 1906. *Scarabs*. London.

Ranke, H., 1935. *Die ägyptischen Personennamen* I. Glückstadt.

Vodoz, Irene., 1978. *Le scarabees gravees du Musée d'Art ed d'Histoire de Geneve*. (Aégyptiaca Helvetica 6). Geneva.

Wilson, J.H., 1951. *The Burden of Egypt*, Chicago.

3

Canaanites in the Eastern Nile Delta

Manfred Bietak

IN the course of excavations at Tell el-Dab'a by the Archaeological Institute of Austria new data have been acquired for our understanding of the origin and nature of Asiatic settlement in the Eastern Nile Delta during the Middle Kingdom and the Second Intermediate Period. The site is now generally identified with Avaris, the capital of the Hyksos and together with Qantir as Piramesse, the Delta capital of the 19th and 20th dynasties. It was situated at the main north-eastern entrance of the Nile Delta. In recent years important evidence of earlier periods in this region has appeared.

Of particular interest is an orthogonal planned settlement of the First Intermediate Period. It was protected by a strong wall and can be considered as an attempt by the kings of Heracleopolis to check the infiltration of Middle Bronze Age I (EB-MB) nomads. It was not, however, those Asiatics who were to influence future events in the north-east of Egypt. During the time of the 12th and even more so during the 13th dynasty, Egypt had intensive trade relations by sea with Syro-Palestinian coastal towns, particularly with Byblos as the principal partner of Egypt in this area. It is from this close relationship that the most likely interpretation of archaeological evidence at Tell el-Dab'a is attempted. Remains of an extensive town site of about 2 sq km

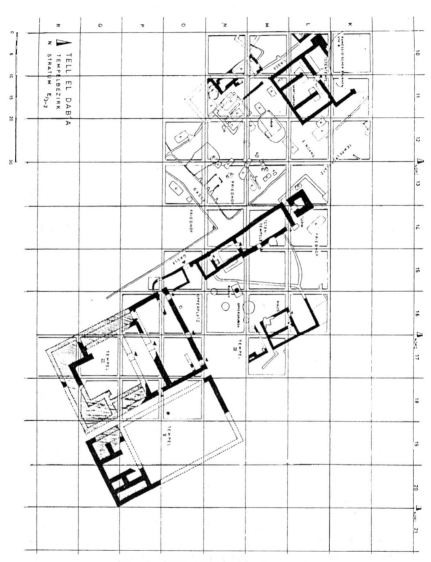

Fig. 1 — Tell el-Dab'a: Temple complex

with a series of strata of occupation of the Syro-Palestinian Middle Bronze Age Culture II A and II B suggest a build-up of a colony of Phoenicians from the area of Byblos from the end of the 12th dynasty onwards. (Pl. A; Fig. 1). It seems very likely now that the site of Tell el-Dab'a had been *the* partner harbor to Byblos through its direct connections to the Mediterranean by the Pelusiac branch and by its ideal harbor facilities. A cylinder seal found on the floor of a palace of the 18th century B.C: in Tell el-Dab'a (Pl. B) shows a representation of the Phoenician god Ba'al Zephon as protector of the sailors.[1]

The distribution of the earliest types of the Tell el-Yehudiyeh ware shows clearly an exclusive representation in coastal Phoenicia down to Megiddo and in northern Egypt (Figs. 2-3). In Palestine other kinds of Tell el-Yehudiyeh ware seem to indicate the formation of another local cultural province with its center in the north (Figs. 4-5). It is important that the distribution of the earlier types of the Tell el-Yehudiyeh ware are clustered exclusively in the Delta and Phoenicia on one hand and in Palestine on the other.

The economic background of the speedily growing Middle Bronze Age town in Tell el-Dab'a was the trade between Egypt and Phoenicia, particularly attested to by an enormous quantity of Canaanite amphoras, but also by other kinds of pottery. This trade soon expanded to Upper Egypt and to Kerma in the Sudan. On the other hand, industry also contributed to the economy, especially the copper industry, stimulated by imports, most likely from Cyprus.

It is not surprising, therefore,.that the cultural appearance of the Middle Bronze Age population in Tell el-Dab'a was not homogeneous. Besides close cultural ties with Phoenicia, other cultural elements were included, in smaller quantities. A local cultural tradition of Cypriote MB-elements can be observed and also some MB-elements from the northern part of Palestine. It should be mentioned in this connection that along with Byblos,

Pl.A — Tell el-Dab'a: Str. G. MBIIA settlement

Pl.B Tell-el Dab'a: site of the Middle Kingdom palace cutting into first intermediate period settlement

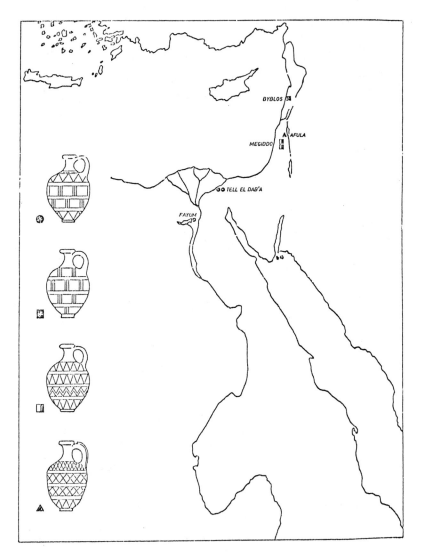

Fig. 2 — Tell el-Yehudiyeh juglets: Earliest Distribution I

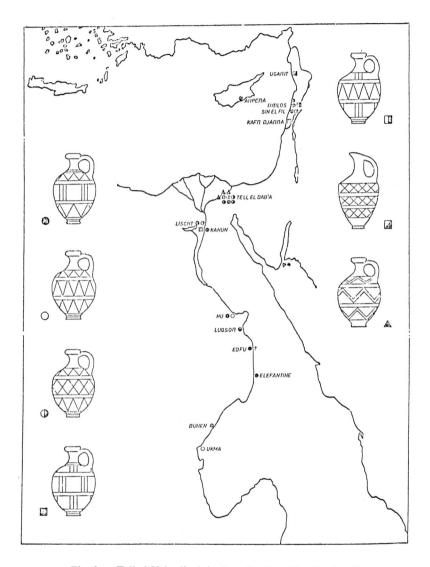

Fig. 3 — Tell el-Yehudiyeh juglets: Earliest Distribution II

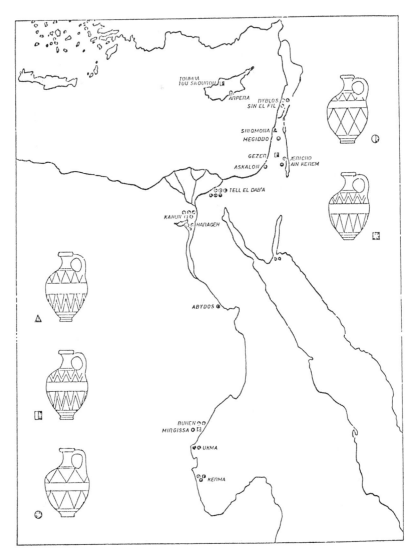

Fig. 4 — Tell el-Yehudiyeh juglets: Local Cultural Province I

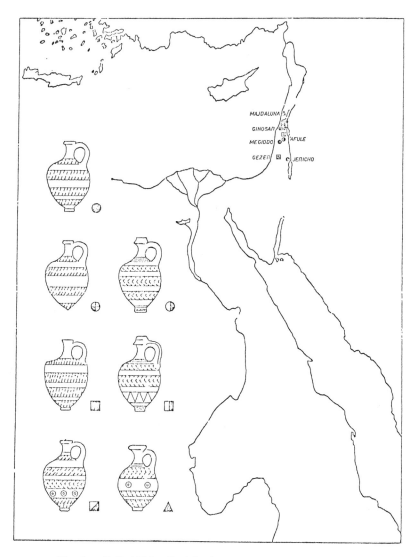

Fig. 5 — Tell el-Yehudiyeh juglets: Local Cultural Province II

some kind of intensive relationship seems to have existed between Middle Kingdom Egypt and Megiddo.

Another important element of this community in Tell el-Dab'a was of course the Egyptian substratum, showing up especially in the burial customs and in the meager funerary outfit. Despite the strong Egyptian cultural influence on the Asiatic settlers, the Egyptian ethnic element seems to have represented the lower class only at the end of the 18th century B.C..[2] On the other hand, Egyptian luxury goods were frequent in the Middle Bronze Age tombs, especially alabaster jars and jewellery.

It was during the time of the late 13th dynasty that local rulers in the Delta became independent. We know that at Avaris, approximately around 1730-1720 B.C., a king Nehesy (or perhaps his father) founded a local kingdom and it is of special interest now that a big palace, obviously a royal residence, appeared among the MB-sequence in Tell el-Dab'a (Pl. C). It is not clear, however, whether it had been a summer residence of an Egyptian king of the 13th dynasty or the palace of a Delta ruler of Asiatic origin. Finds from this palace suggest the latter, although the architecture seems to be Egyptian.

Something must have happened soon afterwards in the first half of the 17th century B.C. While at the center of the town site occupation seems to have been continuous, the eastern part of the town had obviously been abandoned and the plots redistributed along new lines. Family cemeteries started to spread around the big Middle Bronze Age type temple developing into to a big sacred complex which seemed to have been in close relationship to the mortuary cult. Another temple complex was also found in the centre of the town without relationship to burials([1]). Donkey sacrifices and big offering deposits in front of both temples, and also in front of major tombs, reveal rituals characteristic of this MB population. Servants were occasionally buried at the threshold of the tombs of their masters. There is abundant material for the study of the cultural appearance of the

Pl.C — Middle Kingdom palace with scaffolding remains (pits), cutting into a MBIIA settlement. Major pits filled with sand are column foundations.

Middle Bronze Age in the Delta available at Tell el-Dab'a. The cultural background of this MB population was urban rather than nomadic. Indicators in this respect are the intramural burials, a typical urban custom not practised by nomads, and distinct architectural traditions of this culture, e.g., the vaulting technique. The majority of tombs was constructed according to a technique which had a tradition in Mesopotamia, but not in Egypt.[3]

The Middle Bronze Age element in the town site seems to have been increased by a new influx which most likely was responsible for the rise of the Hyksos rule in Egypt. An explanation for this phenomenon can perhaps be found in the close cultural ties between Tell el-Dab'a and Phoenicia, especially Byblos, during the strata G and F. Immediately afterwards we have nearly no MB evidence in Lebanon from the MB II B onwards. The royal tomb series was discontinued about 1720 B.C. and afterwards there seems to be an archaeological blackout. It is only a preliminary opinion now but it seems likely that the conquest of the Kingdom of Mari by Hammurabi of Babylonia and the destruction of the kingdom of Qatna by the kingdom of Yamkhad[4] (Aleppo) towards the end of the 18th century B.C. seriously damaged vital trading routes of Byblos. Those and other disturbances unknown to us may have caused a kind of exodus by Byblites to the Eastern Delta, particularly to Tell el-Dab'a, where their own people had already stongly established themselves on most advantageous terms against the background of the declining late 13th dynasty.

This new influx from Phoenicia would also have caused some reshuffling in the local political scene of the Eastern Delta and it is important for us that the archaeological picture and hypotheses concerning Phoenician origins are last but not least backed up by the Manethonian tradition[5] stressing that the 15th (or the 17th meaning the 15th) dynasty consisted of kings from Phoenicia.

Trade relations were now intensified from the Eastern Delta

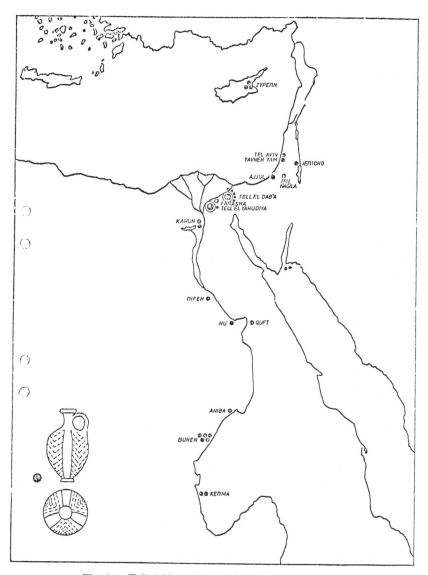

Fig. 6 — Tell el-Yehudiyeh juglets: Ware later types I

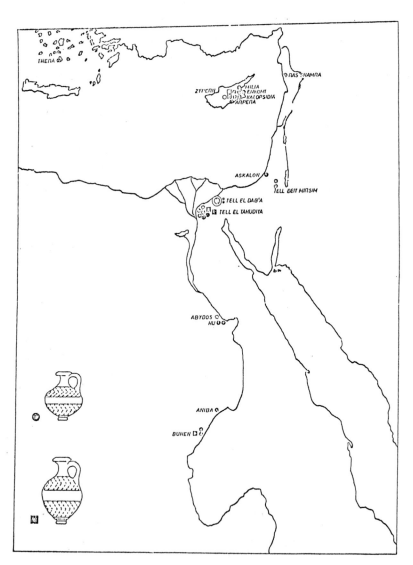

Fig. 7 — Tell el-Yehudiyeh: Juglets: Later types II

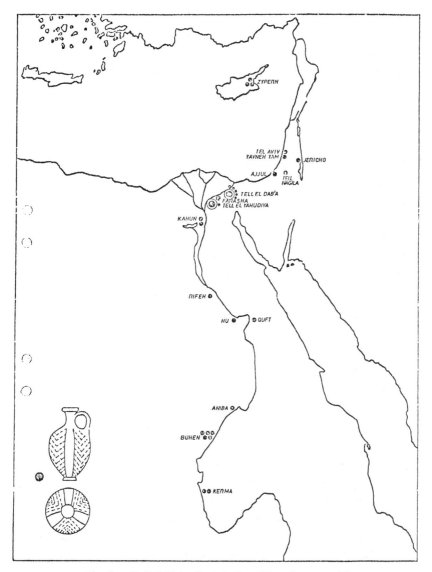

Fig. 6 — Tell el-Yehudiyeh juglets: Ware later types I

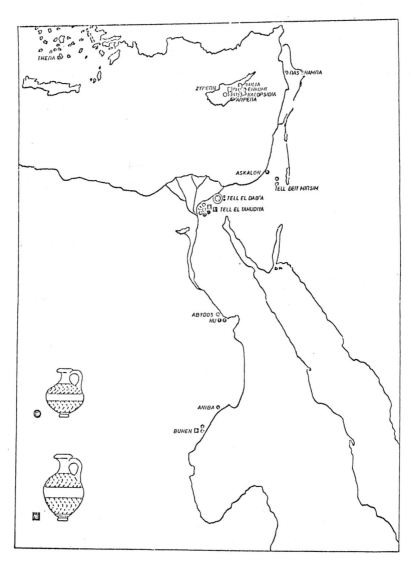

Fig. 7 — Tell el-Yehudiyeh: Juglets: Later types II

to Cyprus and Southern Palestine on the one hand, and Upper Egypt and Kerma on the other. The distribution of the later types of the Tell el-Yehudiyeh ware strongly supports the impression of the formation of a Middle Bronze Age Delta province including Southern Palestine (Tell el-'Ajjul). Some connections were maintained with the rest of Canaan where strong cultural unity had developed while ties with Phoenicia seemed to have ceased to exist (Figs. 6-7). Most of the trade relationship was carried out by sea, and not along the coastal route on the northern coast of Sinai. Sinai has very little Middle Bronze Age evidence according to intensive surveys carried out by E. Oren.[6] Also the numerous bulky Canaanite amphoras from the 13th dynasty and the Second Intermediate Period found in Tell el-Dab'a and Northern Egypt exclude serious considerations of the land trading route.

Towards the end of the Second Intermediate Period trade relations between Tell el-Dab'a and the former partners like Nubia, Upper Egypt and Cyprus declined considerably, as revealed by the pottery analysis. It seems that Thebans, former vassals to the Hyksos, strangled the important trading routes to the South. So there was little available in exchange for trade with Cyprus and the Mediterranean. This caused economic weakness and the decline of the Hyksos kingdom in the North.

NOTES

1   According to an investigation by Prof. E. Parada, Columbia University.
2   At one place on the site, they seemed to have been the victims of a plague as indicated by multiple burials.
3   According to a thesis by Dr. C.M. van den Brink.
4   Already suggested by Mazar (1968:86-87).
5   Africanus' and Eusebius' version and Scholia to Plato.
6   Personal communication by E. Oren, in: Rothenberg 1979:112; and Oren 1973:198-205.

REFERENCES

Mazar, B., 1968. The Middle Bronze Age in Palestine. *IEJ* 18:65-97.

Oren, E.D., 1973. The Overland Route between Egypt and Canaan in the Early Bronze Age. *IEJ* 23:198-205.

Rothenberg, B., 1979. *Sinai.* Bern.

4

Canaanites and Egyptians at Serabit el-Khadim

Itzhaq Beit-Arieh

EVER since the discovery of the Egyptian temple at Serabit el-Khadim (Fig. 1; Pl. A) by C. Niebuhr in 1762, research concerning it has focused around two subjects: the temple itself with its numerous inscribed stelae and the corpus of Proto-Sinaitic inscriptions, some of which were found within the temple compound, although most of them came from in and around the turquoise mines in the vicinity.

This article is concerned with these Proto-Sinaitic inscriptions, which have a direct bearing on Canaanite-Egyptian relations in the relevant period, and particularly with the new evidence on the subject that we had the good fortune to discover in the course of our investigation.

Regarding the inscriptions: it is significant that one-third of them (out of a total of about 35) are located in Mines M and L. The first was discovered by E.H. Palmer in 1869, others by Sir Flinders Petrie during his explorations of Serabit el-Khadim in 1905 and additional ones were brought to light by the 1927, 1930 and 1935 expeditions of Harvard University and others. In 1935 the Harvard expedition excavated Mine M, not only in quest of additional inscriptions but to try and find some datable evidence in order to determine to which of the two periods of Egyptian

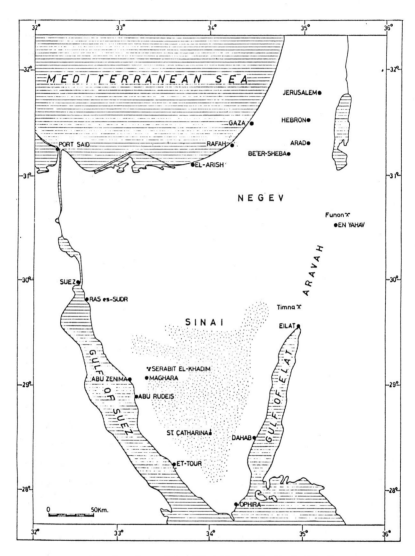

Fig. 1 — Location of Serabit el-Khadim in Sinai.

activity in the region — the Middle Kingdom or the Late Kingdom — these inscriptions should be assigned.

Although the Harvard expedition recovered a number of stone artifacts and pottery sherds from the mine, these were undatable, and aside from enriching the corpus of Proto-Sinaitic inscriptions, it did not make any progress in its endeavours to determine their date (Starr and Butin 1936). Consequently, we find scholars such as Gardiner, Butin and Sethe, who assign the inscriptions to the Middle Kingdom, whereas Petrie, Albright and Cross date them to the New Kingdom (Gardiner 1962:45-48; Butin 1932:133-134; Sethe 1917:437-475; Petrie 1906:131-132; Albright 1969; Cross 1967:12.

Recently new evidence that may help to solve the problem has been discovered in an excavation of the Ophir Expedition to Sinai, sponsored by the Institute of Archaeology of Tel Aviv University and directed by the author.

THE EXCAVATIONS

Our excavations, which lasted three weeks in 1977-1978, were concentrated in Mine L, adjacent to Mine M, which was explored by the Harvard Expedition. Mine L, as we know it today, has two large chambers connected to each other by a narrow tunnel (Pl.B). Branching off from these chambers at different levels are the galleries where the turquoise veins were quarried. Most of the gallery floors are covered with heaps of mining debris. During our excavations we cleared the eastern part of the southern chamber systematically down to bedrock. Amongst the debris we discovered a smoothed slab of Nubian sandstone incised with two Proto-Sinaitic characters: *'alef* and *lamed* ("El"). The inscription, which reads vertically, is bordered at the right-hand side by a vertical groove and at the bottom by a horizontal groove; since the space above and to the left of the letters was left blank, these two letters are apparently the complete inscription,

Pl.A — The temple of Ḥatḥor: General view

Pl.B — Serabit el-Khadim. Mine L, general view

which consists solely of the name of the god El, the chief divinity of the Northwest Semitic pantheon.

Although such a find was not unexpected, particularly in this mine, which had yielded other Pro-Sinaitic inscriptions in the past, the finds from the lower level of the gallery were most surprising. This was a collection of metallurgical objects (Pl.C) that included 47 open molds of Nubian sandstone for casting bronze tools, the base of a bellows hewn from a single block of stone (Pl.D), clay nozzles (tuyeres) for delivering the air blast from the bellows to the furnace, several clay crucibles and lumps of melted bronze.

Most of the molds are for casting mining tools, including axes, scrapers, chisels and knives, but there are also a few for mirrors and ingots. A thin film of copper residue still adheres to some of the molds (For color photographs of several of the finds, see Beit-Arieh 1984:44-46).

This is the largest assemblage of metal-casting molds ever discovered in the ancient Near East. Prototypes of some of the tools can be traced back to the fifth millennium. Analogies to the stone bellows (whose opening was originally fitted with an inflatable leather bag), are known in the third millennium in northern Syria and the first half of the second millennium in Canaan, while in Egypt the famous 18th Dynasty wall painting from the tomb of Rekh-Mi-Ré at Thebes (Davies 1943: Pl. LII) depicts coppersmiths at their work, each pumping with his feet a pair of bellows that are identical to ours.

During our explorations around Serabit el-Khadim and our survey of the southern slope of the plateau, two previously unknown Proto-Sinaitic inscriptions were discovered at the entrance to Mine G. (Pl.E) Just above the mine-shaft there was another assemblage of metal-working equipment, including an additional foot-operated bellows, clay tuyeres and crucibles similar to those discovered in Mine L. Undoubtedly, this equipment all belonged to metal-smiths who were attached to the royal Egyptian mining

Pl.C — An axe head mold. Found in Mine L.

Pl.D — Base of a foot bellows as it was found in Mine L.

expedition stationed at the site. The miners' tools were most likely made of bronze, and when damaged, they were apparently remelted by the metal-smiths, and new tools cast on the spot in order to avoid delays in the quarrying operations.

DISCUSSION

Since our primary goal was to determine the date of the Proto-Sinaitic inscriptions, it is worthwhile to deal with this aspect of the research in some detail, before entering into the question of the nature of the relations between the Egyptian officials of the mining expedition and the identity of the workers attached to it. The archaeological evidence, which falls into three categories, points to a date in the New Kingdom.

1) *Ceramic*: Although very little pottery was recovered, a sherd of Bichrome ware, which is typical of the Late Bronze Age ceramic repertoire in Canaan, was found in Mine L, while a faience vessel decorated in a geometric pattern common in Egypt in the New Kingdom came from Mine G.

2) *Metallurgic*: One of the casting molds from Mine L is for a type of axe that was known in Egypt mainly during the New Kingdom (Davies 1943: Pl. LII; Petrie 1917: Pls. II:93-94; VII:144, 151-152).

3) *Stone bellows*: Depictions of foot-operated bellows similar to those discovered in the mines are known from several wall paintings in the tombs of Theban nobles, all of which are dated to the New Kingdom (Fig. 2). Similar objects were found in late Middle Bronze Age contexts in Canaan, two in Stratum D at Tell Beit Mirsim and another from the same period at Lachish (Albright 1938:53-54; Ussishkin 1983:108-109). In northern Syria they are known already in the second half of the third millennium (Davey 1979). Their geographical-chronological distribution therefore seems to indicate a northern origin and a slow dispersal southwards.

Significantly, the only mines in the Serabit el-Khadim region

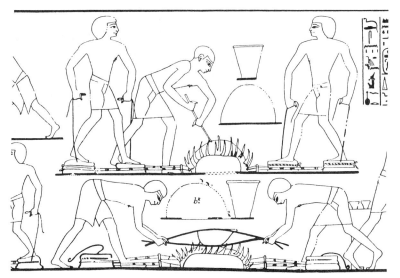

Fig. 2 — Coppersmiths using foot bellows. A wall painting from
the tomb of Rekh-Mi-Ré.

Pl.E — Serabit el-Khadim: A plaque with a Proto-Sinaitic inscription, "El".
Found in Mine L.

in which both Proto-Sinaitic inscriptions and metallurgical equipment were found are Mines G, L, and M, which is a good indication that the equipment and inscriptions are contemporaneous. Obviously, if the metallurgical equipment can be dated to the final period of Egyptian activity at the site (the New Kingdom) this is strong evidence for assigning the Proto-Sinaitic inscriptions to the same period. It should be remembered that several of the inscribed slabs found at the beginning of the century were strewn on the surface outside the mine shafts, additional evidence that they belong to the final phase of Egyptian presence at the site.

Two important objectives of our research at Serabit el-Khadim were to establish the ethnic identify of the writers of the Proto-Sinaitic inscriptions and the geographical origin of the coppersmiths mentioned in the Egyptian hieroglyphic inscriptions of the temple and whose equipment is described above. Were these the same people? Since the hieroglyphic inscriptions do not reveal anything regarding the origin of the coppersmiths, it is not impossible that they were Egyptians like the rest of the members of the mining expedition. However, the general consensus (Albright 1969) is that the Proto-Sinaitic inscriptions were the work of the same Asiatics that are mentioned on the temple stelae. The fact that identical alphabetic symbols were already used in Canaan in the 19th century B.C.E. not only points to the specific locale of their origin but completely eliminates the possibility (as suggested in the past) that the alphabet was invented in southern Sinai (Cross 1967).

To return to the subject of this article: What was the status of these Canaanites and their relation to the Egyptian officials of the expedition? Since workers with Semitic names are mentioned in several of the hieroglyphic stelae of the Middle and New Kingdoms, including a "brother of the governor of Retjenu," it seems very likely that these Asiatics were of independent status (Černy 1935:389), artisans who arrived at this niming center deep in the heart of Sinai of their own free will and initiative (and not slaves or forced laborers, as sometimes suggested in the past). This would not be a new phenomenon in the history of the Canaanites. There is evidence of population movements to Sinai from the fourth millenium onwards, including miners and metal-smiths (Beit-Arieh 1980; 1983). Since it is natural for metal-smiths to migrate to mining centers, it seems to us that of all the possible professions of the Canaanites in Sinai, the most logical would be metal working, a craft of ancient tradition amongst the peoples that populated the Land of Israel in various periods of its history.

REFERENCES

Albright, W.F., 1938. The Excavation of Tell Beit Mirsim: The Bronze Age. *AASOR* 17.

Albright, W.F., 1969. *The Proto-Sinaitic Inscriptions and their Decipherment* (rvsd. 2nd ed.). Cambridge (Mass).

Beit-Arieh, I., 1980. A Chalcolithic Site near Serabit el-Khadim. *Tel Aviv* 7:45-64.

Beit-Arieh, I., 1983. Central-Southern Sinai in the Early Bronze II and its Relationship with Palestine. *Levant* 15:39-48.

Beit-Arieh, I., 1984. Fifteen Years in Sinai. *Biblical Archaeology Review* 10(4):26-54.

Butin, R.F., 1932. The Serabit Expedition of 1930: The Proto-Sinaitic Inscriptions. *Harvard Theological Review* 25:130-203.

Černy, J., 1935. Semites in Egyptian Mining Expeditions to Sinai. *Archiv Orientalni* 7:384-389.

Cross, F.M., Jr. 1967. The Origin and Early Evolution of the Alphabet. *Eretz-Israel* 8:8-24.

Davey, C.J., 1979. Some Ancient Near Eastern Pot Bellows. *Levant* 11:101-111.

Davies, N. de G. 1943. *Tomb of Rekh-Mi-Re at Thebes II*. New York.

Gardiner, A., 1962. Once Again the Proto-Sinaitic Inscriptions. *JEA* 48:45-48.

Petrie, W.M.F., 1906. *Researches in Sinai*. London.

Petrie, W.M.F., 1917. *Tools and Weapons*. London.

Sethe, K., 1917. Die Neuentoleckte Sinai-schrift und die Entstehung der semitischen Schrift. *Nachrichten von der K. Gesellschaft der Wissenschaften 30*. Göttingen: 437-475.

Starr, R.F.S., and Butin, R.F., 1936. Excavations and Proto-Sinaitic Inscriptions at Serabit el-Khadim. *Studies and Documents VI*. London.

5

The "Ways of Horus" in North Sinai

Eliezer D. Oren

O NE of the most dramatic chapters in the history of Egypt and Canaan began with the fall of Avaris, the Hyksos Capital in the Delta, and the conquest of the Hyksos strongholds in southern Canaan. Subsequent military campaigns into Canaan by the kings of the early XVIIIth Dynasty, particularly the expeditions of Thutmose III (1504-1450 B.C.E.), paved the way for the establishment of the Egyptian empire of the New Kingdom, that held sway for almost three hundred years over the entire area between the fourth cataract of the Nile and the Euphrates River. Numerous contemporary documents, coupled with the rich archaeological record from Egypt and Canaan, provide a detailed picture of Egypt's foreign policy and of the close commercial and cultural contacts between Egypt and its provinces to the east (Weinstein 1981:18-21). The first direct references to North Sinai appear in documents of the New Kingdom, clarifying its importance in the geopolitical system of the Egyptian empire.

During the New Egyptian Kingdom the coastal strip of northern Sinai became the major land-bridge over which the military and commercial traffic between Egypt and Asia flowed. The route along the Mediterranean coast of Sinai known in the Egyptian sources as "The Ways of Horus," after its first station on the eastern frontier, was the vital and efficient artery through which Egypt communicated with her Asian province.[1] Judging from the Egyptian documents and recent archaeological discoveries, it is evident that Egypt's interests in this inhospitable land were secured by a network of forts and supply and customs stations that were established along it, between the eastern Delta and southern Canaan. Indeed, Thutmose III's first campaign from the border fortress of Sile to Gaza, about 250 km away, in the record time of a mere nine to ten days testifies to the effectiveness of Egypt's organization in the "Ways of Horus" (Wilson 1955:235).

The rebuilding of the military occupation in North Sinai, on a scale far surpassing what had existed previously, is probably to be assigned to Seti I who conducted punitive expeditions against the nomadic tribes in Sinai and was responsible for renewing Egypt's control in Canaan, in an area extending from Sile on the eastern frontier to Upi in the Damascus area. The subsequent reigns of Merneptah (1223-1213 B.C.E.) and of his successors Seti II and Twosret (1199-1185 B.C.E.) mark, according to many scholars, a period of weak control over Sinai and Canaan — perhaps even the end of Egypt's powerful presence there (Faulkner 1975:217-251; Kitchen 1982:215-216). Nevertheless, the latter rulers, in particular Seti II, are represented by a number of monuments in Egypt proper, near the turquoise and copper mines in Sinai and the Arabah and at sites in Canaan (Rothenberg 1972:163; Fig. 49:6; Faulkner 1975:237). Egyptian administration in Canaan was restored briefly by Ramesses III, but had soon declined entirely in the international arena and by the time of Ramesses V or VI, had retreated to its old border in the Delta.[2]

In 1920 Sir Alan Gardiner published a detailed study entitled "The Ancient Military Road Between Egypt and Palestine" where he systematically analysed most of the available sources concerning the "Ways of Horus" during the New Kingdom

(Gardiner 1920:99-116). The two most important documents on this subject are Papyrus Anastasi I from the reign of Ramesses II, and the reliefs on the north wall of the great Hypostyle Hall in the temple of Amun at Karnak from the time of Seti I. The papyrus, a kind of "geographic guide" written in a satiric language, lists the stations in North Sinai as well as the major fortified cities in southern Canaan (Wilson 1955:475-479). The Karnak reliefs, on the other hand, record graphically the first campaign of Seti I into Sinai and beyond, and his victorious return to Egypt (Fig. 1). The depiction in the Karnak reliefs of the stations and forts along the "Ways of Horus", most likely commemorated the renewal of Egypt's military and adminis-trative presence in North Sinai at the beginning of the XIXth Dynasty.

The opening statement in the Karnak reliefs "...the destruction made by the mighty arm of the Pharaoh amongst the fallen enemies of the Shasu, from the fortress of the Thel (Sile) and to the [city of] Canaan [Gaza]", implies that prior to the major thrust into Canaan, Seti was obliged to undertake punitive actions against the Shasu, the Bedouin tribes of the North Sinai, in order to secure the Egyptian border and control the road across the desert (Faulkner 1947:34-40). The reliefs represent the campaign from east to west in three related scenes, in the center of which stands the enlarged, imposing figure of Seti in his chariot. Egypt is separated from the Sinai desert by a canal running south-north, whose crocodile-infested waters and reed-lined banks are characteristic of fresh water environment (cf. Fig. 1, upper right). This canal, called *Ta-denit*, namely "the dividing waters" or simply "the canal" runs diagonally into another body of water that brims with fish — the salt water of the Mediterranean. The canal should probably be identified with the traces of an ancient waterway discovered recently in the region between Pelusium and Qantara (Fig. 2) (Sneh and Weissbrod 1973:59-61; Sneh *et al.* 1975:542-548; Shea 1977:31-

Fig. 1 — Stations and forts along the "Ways of Horus". Relief on the north wall
of the great Hypostyle Hall in the temple of Amun at Karnak.

38). It served as a major source of fresh water to the edge of the eastern Nile Delta and an important artery for maritime traffic as well as effectively closing the eastern border to nomadic infiltrations and invading armies. This "frontier canal" would also be in keeping with the historical geography of the Delta during the empire period, when the chief political and administrative center had shifted from Thebes to Pi-Ramesse, the new royal residence of the XIXth Dynasty in the eastern Nile Delta.

Of the twenty stations listed in both Papyrus Anastasi I and the Karnak reliefs it is possible to identify with a degree of certainty only Gaza, called "the [city of] Canaan" and Raphia on the Canaanite terminus of the "Ways of Horus" and perhaps also Sile and Migdol on the eastern border of Egypt.[3] The remaining stations took the names or epithets of Seti I and Ramesses II and consequently are impossible to identify with any specific site.[4] In any case, regardless of where these stations were once located it is not unlikely that the similarity between the lists of stations named in these two sources, points to a common origin, perhaps an itinerary or even an early map, that included detailed information on the course of the road as well as on the stations along the way.

The eleven forts and nine wells, or water reservoirs, that line the "Ways of Horus" are depicted between the horse's feet and the wheels of Seti I's chariot. The crucial question is obviously whether the Karnak relief is to be regarded as a reliable "map" of the "Ways of Horus," or merely as a schematic representation of forts and wells whose size and location in the scenes were determined by artistic conventions or constraints, such as the amount of space which remained after the artist had completed the central scene of Pharaoh charging with his chariots, the battle, the files of captives etc. The seemingly detailed portrayal of wells and water reservoirs and the varying scale and plan of the forts could argue that these reliefs are a realistic visual record

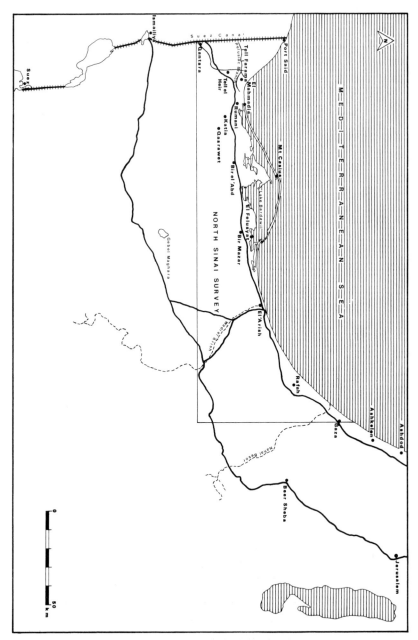

Fig. 2 — Ancient waterways and New Kingdom sites in the Eastern Delta

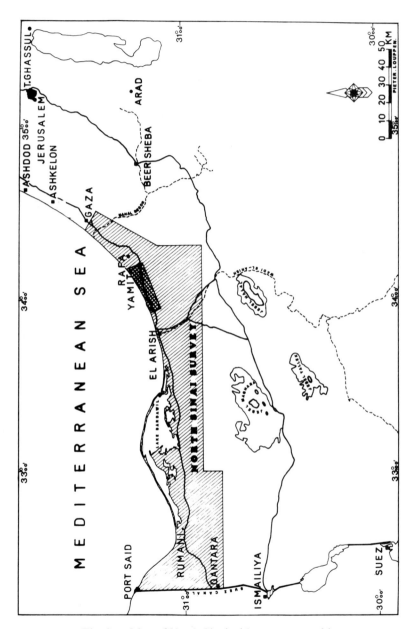

Fig. 3 — Map of North Sinai with area surveyed by
Ben-Gurion University expedition

of the region. This intriguing question will have to be considered below in the light of the new archaeological evidence unearthed by our expedition in the North Sinai.

The historical sources concerning the "Ways of Horus" in North Sinai indicated an extremely well organized system of forts and road stations established by the Pharaohs of the New Kingdom to secure the major artery of communication with the Asiatic provinces. Yet, despite its immense importance, this chapter of Egyptian history has remained until recently a *terra incognita* to archaeological scholarship. This state of research is perhaps best illustrated by Sir Alan Gardiner's classic study where he carefully examined the available written sources for the identification of the forts and stations along the ancient highway in northern Sinai. However, the location of these forts, and consequently the alignment of the ancient highway, was not founded on any archaeological evidence whatsoever. Similarly, twenty years of surveys and excavations (1904-1924) in the eastern Nile Delta and along the Mediterranean coast of Sinai by Jean Cledat have yielded valuable data on the history of the region in Roman and Byzantine times but, except for one site of the Protodynastic period, no archaeological remains earlier than the Hellenistic were reported. As a result the reconstruction of Egypt's administrative and military organization along the "Ways of Horus" was founded, until recently, almost entirely on literary sources and a few accidental or sporadic archaeological discoveries.[5]

From 1972 to 1982 the Ben Gurion University expedition, under the direction of the present author, explored more than eighty New Kingdom settlement sites in the coastal and sand-duned area between the Suez Canal and Gaza (Figs. 3-4). The survey results enable us for the first time to delineate the course of the "Ways of Horus" in accurate detail, and to reconstruct the history of settlement and the degree of Egyptian activity on that land bridge between the Delta and southern Canaan.[6] The largest concentration of New Kingdom sites is reported in the south-western corner of Sinai, in the triangle formed by Port Said, Rumani and Qantara. These sites are represented by industrial and domestic installations. Some of the larger settlements yielded building remains in stone and brick, including sections of granite columns that probably belonged to some public structures. The recently discovered ancient canal flowing through this region made it part of the fertile and densely populated eastern Delta. The occurrence of New Kingdom sites along the eastern "frontier canal" argues that the construction of this ambitious project was effected during the New Kingdom at the latest.

East of the Delta plain and south of the Bardawil Lagoon we recorded New Kingdom sites in an area roughly parallel to the modern road and railway line between Raphia and Qantara.[7] We should stress here that there were almost no New Kingdom sites on the coast, nor on the sand bar enclosing the Bardawil Lagoon to the north; making it highly probable that the settlements were cut off from direct maritime traffic. The latter observation is of immense importance for the study of the historical geography of North Sinai during the New Kingdom period.[8]

The distribution map of settlement in the New Kingdom is characterized by clusters of sites in which the central fort, or station, is surrounded by many smaller camp sites for caravans, and by many seasonal encampments for the local inhabitants who lived in huts or in tents and depended for their protection and supplies on the Egyptian authorities in the main settlement. We recorded clusters like these in at least ten different places between the Suez Canal and Raphia, including the eastern Delta and the regions of Rumani, Nagila, Bir el-'Abd, Madba'a, El Mazar, El 'Arish, and Haruba. Numerous New Kingdom sites were also encountered by our expedition between Raphia and Gaza. To this we may add the late Bronze Age settlement remains at Tell Abu Salima, Tell Riddan and Deir el-Balah.

The following chapter will focus on three types of sites that the

North Sinai Expedition explored most intensively: Bir el-'Abd and two sites in the Haruba area. They represent Egypt's manifold activities along the "Ways of Horus": i.e., military, administrative and industrial.

The cluster at Bir el-'Abd consisted of a central site (BEA-10 on the expedition map) surrounded in a radius of 3 to 4 km by a dense grouping of some thirty small encampments, usually located in the shallow, interduned areas.[9] The remains at these settlements were extremely poor, including only fragments of hearths, refuse pits, stone grinders and pounders, large quantities of pottery and a few metal objects. The interrelationship of the central site and its satellites is reflected in the close similarity of their ceramic assemblages: a great deal of Egyptian pottery, a few Canaanite containers, and fragments of imported Cypriote and Aegean pottery vessels. At one site, C-68, we recovered a relatively large collection of Mycenaean and Cypriote pottery.

Site BEA-10 extends over an area of about 50 dunams, although the actual remains of buildings do not cover an area larger than 5 dunams, or just over one acre. Excavations in the central part of the site, Area A, revealed the remains of massive mud-brick walls, constructed in a technique typical of Egyptian brick architecture. The few preserved sections of beaten earth floors yielded scores of Egyptian vessels: bowls, storage jars, jar stands, and decorated vessels of characteristic New Kingdom types. The architectural remains in Area A included poorly preserved thick walls of a monumental structure, seemingly a fort that stood in the central part of the site and extended over an area of 1600 sqm. The large courtyard contained brick installations for cooking, baking, and storage, hearths, and refuse pits; and a considerable deposit of animal and fish bones. The wide, shallow depression lying to the south of Area A was scattered with broken pottery vessels, basalt and granite grinders and pounders. Clearly, this was the settlement's dump.

The southern section, Area B, yielded the remains of an

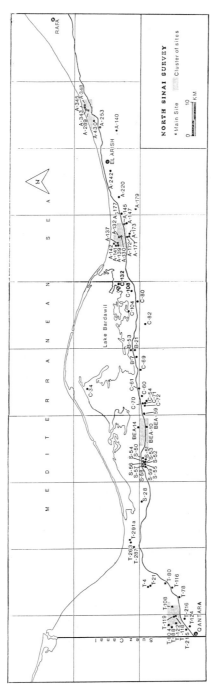

Fig. 4 — Map of North Sinai survey with LBA-NK sites and clusters

impressive granary and, to the west of it, a complex of magazines. The granary is composed of four cylindrical silos, each about 4 m in circumference, with walls approximately 50 cm. thick (Pl.A). Two of the silos contained projecting shelves, one brick thick; these may have marked the location of the opening, which was just above the outside ground level. Both floors and walls had been covered with a generous layer of plaster.

Silos 2 and 3 are preserved up to the level of the openings only, A section of Silo 4 still included at least four courses of the dome, which enabled us to reconstruct the entire structure and the method used to build it. The dome was corbelled, with alternating rings of bricks set either flat or upright and the spaces between the courses were filled in with cement, creating the impression of a true dome. The Bir el-'Abd granary could have held up to 44,600 liters, or about 40 tons of grain. On the floor of three of the silos, there was a thin layer of organic material, probably grain, buried beneath quantities of broken pottery vessels, alabaster, faience vessels and many animal and fish bones. Judging from the refuse deposits that cover the layer of brick material from the collapsed dome in each of the Silos, they must have served as refuse pits for the inhabitants of the fort after they ceased to function as granaries.

Further poor remains of brick structures were explored about 20 meters west of the fort. Here the remaining elongated halls, fronted by wide open courtyards, must be interpreted as magazines. The inner walls of these structures were often supported by brick buttresses, as were the openings. At Haruba, site A-345, which will be described below, our expedition discovered structures similar in plan to the Bir el-'Abd magazines and identical in building method, down to the size of the individual bricks and the bonding pattern.

Granary and grain magazine complexes are well documented in New Kingdom Egypt and appear to be very popular subjects in Egyptian wall paintings and in miniature models of daily

Pl. A — Granary in Site BEA 10

activities (Fig. 5).[10] Such installations were usually isolated from the rest of the settlement by an enclosure wall, and the filling and emptying of silos was closely supervised and monitored by Egyptian officials. The new data from Bir el-'Abd now enable us to evaluate the effectiveness of the administrative arrangements for provisioning and serving the caravans and particularly military expeditions that traversed the "Ways of Horus" in North Sinai by examining the size and structure of the armies, the methods of supply, and troop rations. The participation of some 20,000 soldiers and probably also thousands of service personnel in the battle of Kadesh, for example, gives us some idea of the size of the armies that crossed the "Ways of Horus" and the quantities of provisions they must have had at their disposal.[11]

At the edge of Area A, about 200 m from the remains of the fort, we observed an artificial rectangular-shaped depression in the surface. It measured about 10 m x 15 m and was bordered by a kind of embankment composed of layers of dark silt. The

Fig. 5 — Granary, Tomb of Pehsukhet, Thebes

soundings in this depression revealed that the bottom of the depression and its sides had been intentionally lined with thick layers of muddy silt or clay. The silt contained fragments of New Kingdom pottery. The depression was probably a reservoir designed to collect rain water and may also have been filled with water drawn from neighborhood wells. The waterproofing layers of clay that lined the sides and bottom of the reservoir kept the water from seeping into the sand. A comparable method for collecting water in sand-duned areas is still in use, on a much smaller scale, at some of the Bedouin encampments in North Sinai. Recently a large-scale reservoir was excavated at the Late Bronze Age site of Deir el-'Balah, but thick layers of ash, rather than clay, were used as a water-proof lining (Dothan 1981:127-129). The evidence from these sites enhances our understanding of how water was collected in the stations along the "Ways of Horus." In the reliefs in the temple of Amun at Karnak, the reservoirs and pools are located next to the forts, with palm trees growing nearby. The various configurations of the installations depicted in the reliefs may reflect that their shape was determined by the terrain of the particular station.

The rich collection of the finds from Bir el-'Abd included a large store of Egyptian pottery, with many examples of decorated wares characteristic of late XVIIIth Dynasty styles (fourteenth century B.C.E.). Particularly noteworthy was a group of bowls and drop-shaped vessels of the "Egyptian blue" class, that were painted with blue, red, and black pigments and bearing such Egyptian motifs as the "Eye of Horus" and geometric designs (Pl.B). The site contained hundreds of examples of open vessels shaped like flower pots with very thick, thumb-indented bases.[12] Some of the smaller vessels were decorated with the heads of gazelles, modeled in clay and affixed to the handles (cf. Brunton and Engelbach 1927: Pl. XXXIX:82W; Hayes 1959: Fig. 150, upper right).

It is worth noting that the ceramic collection from Bir el-'Abd is represented by a markedly few Canaanite types, such as cooking pots and storage jars. There were imported Cypriote wares, as well as a few examples of Mycenaean pottery. Fragments of Egyptian alabaster and faience vessels were also collected along with bronze spearheads and arrowheads. The site yielded Egyptian scarabs and seal impressions from the XVIIIth Dynasty, as well as a jar handle impressed with the cartouche of Seti I, who figured so prominently in re-establishing Egyptian domination over the "Ways of Horus" (Pl.C).

Between 1979 and 1982, our expedition explored the important complex of New Kingdom sites in the region of Haruba.[13] The Haruba sites, some twenty in number, are clustered in a relatively small area about 4-5 sq km in the coastal sand-duned region, approximately 12 km east of el-'Arish. The entire area is blanketed by active coastal sand dunes that are separated by wide depressions in which thick groves of palm trees flourish. Our explorations were focused on two particularly impressive sites: A-289, a military fort, and A-345, an administrative center. Both were unusually well-preserved and stand as models of Egyptian civil and military architecture on the "Ways of Horus". One of the encampment sites in the vicinity, A-343, is surrounded on every side by high, active sand dunes. In the center of A-343, we recorded a group of stone installations for baking and cooking, and quantities of restorable pottery vessels of Egyptian, Canaanite and Cypriote types. Two of those vessels proved to be especially interesting. One is a very elegant jug of the Cypriote Base Ring class (cf. Astrom 1972: Fig. XLIX:10). The second, of which we recovered two specimens, is a type of vessel known as the Egyptian "beer bottle" which was stamped with cartouche of Seti I (Pl.D); cf. Brunton and Engelbach 1927: Pl. XXXVIII:53C; Oren 1985: Fig. 7:1). Although the fabric of the vessel indicated that it was produced locally, its shape and technical details were typically Egyptian. These "beer bottles" are welcome testimony to the presence in northern Sinai of official potters' workshops

Pl. B — Egyptian blue painted
vase from granary, Site BEA 10

Pl. C — Jar handle with
cartouche of Seti I,
Site BEA 10

Pl. D — Egyptian "beer bottle" stamped with cartouche of Seti I,
Site A-343

from the time of Seti I, who evidently reorganized Egypt's administration in the "Ways of Horus".

The fort of Haruba was built on the surface of a consolidated sand dune approximately 3/4 acre in size, lying in the midst of active sand dunes. The actual structure of the fort extends over some 2500 sq m. (Fig. 6) Its general plan comprises a massive enclosure wall, a gatehouse, a wide courtyard, and a complex of compartments, including magazines that were built against the outer wall. The enclosure wall is about 4 m wide and was preserved to approximately 1 m in height. On the north wall and at the northeastern corner, we uncovered huge buttresses, some 4 m wide, which may be the bases of watchtowers. The whole structure must have risen at least 6 m. The standard size of the bricks, 45 x 22 x 12 cm and the bonding pattern are typical of public and domestic architecture in Egypt during the New Kingdom (Spencer 1979:104-106). The bricks in the foundation course were typically laid upright on their narrow end, whereas the second course consisted of alternating headers and stretchers. We recorded this style of bricklaying at a number of other New Kingdom sites in northern Sinai, and we have no doubt that such official building operations were undertaken by the Egyptian administration responsible for the "Ways of Horus". Both the size of the building and the building techniques employed bear witness to mastery over engineering problems and to the excellent local administration that, besides providing the necessary tools and materials, supervised the workers.[14] The only entrance to the fort, an impressive gatehouse approximately 13mx12m, protruded from the fort's eastern enclosure wall. The entry way, some 16 m long and 3.70 m wide, is broad enough to allow for the passage of chairiots; the two massive buttresses, 8mx13m, that flank the entrance make the gateway into a solidly fortified unit. Within the buttresses there are two hollow shafts or cells, but the shafts could be entered from above, probably through a system of scaffoldings or wooden ladders, and were used for storage.

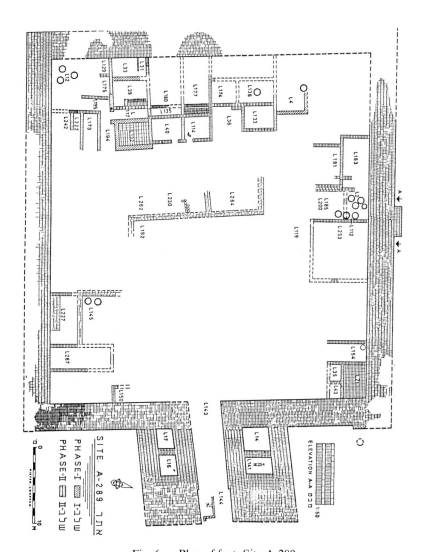

Fig. 6 — Plan of fort, Site A-289

Casemate walls — that is, walls or buttresses that contain empty cells — are well known in Egyptian architecture.[15]

In the outer casemate of the northern buttress (Chamber L-141), we excavated a complete adult male skeleton lying supine on the floor, oriented to the north (Pl. E). Its arms were extended above its head; the head was covered with broken storage jars, around which were deposits of ash, perhaps the remains of a burial custom. In the passageway between the buttresses, we could discern two building phases. The floor of the earlier phase (phase III) was beaten earth reinforced with brick material; in its center a narrow and shallow channel 30 cm wide, filled with ash, had been constructed. The channel apparently was designed to allow for drainage and to carry sewage. Sections of brick pavement, about 2.40 m wide, were constructed at both ends of the gateway to provide a solid base for the wooden doors, that were probably hinged at this point, on either side of the passageway. The excavations yielded stratigraphic evidence of drastic architectural changes in the gateway during its last phase (phase II). The passageway was narrowed to about half its original width by a brick partition wall 20 cm wide constructed on its eastern end to enclose a variety of clay installations for cooking and storage. These changes indicate that in the last phase of the fort, the gateway could not have functioned as a major entry way, for there was not enough room for chariots to pass. The various installations and deposits of ash probably made it unsuitable for animals and pedestrians as well; it may even have gone completely out of use and been replaced by a new entry way at some other point in the enclosure wall. Further evidence that the gateway was obsolete in phase II was confirmed by the discovery of the skeleton of a child at the western end of the gateway.

Aproximately a third of the fort was clear of any structures, perhaps to allow room to pitch tents and park chariots and carts. Soundings in the fort's eastern wing and in front of the gateway

Pl. E — Burial in gate complex of fort, Site A-289

Pl. F — Fragments of Egyptian pithos incised with cartouches of Seti II,
Site A-289

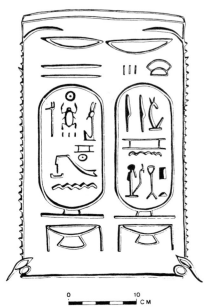

Fig. 7 — Reconstruction of cartouches of Seti II

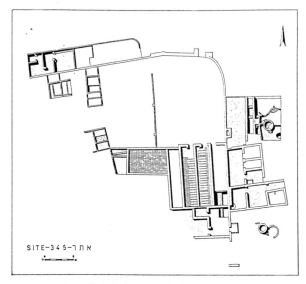

Fig. 8 — Plan of Site A-345

did not produce any building remains, but installations for cooking and pockets of ash were found. The rest of the space inside the walled area was occupied by a large number of rooms whose walls abutted the enclosure wall and opened into the courtyard. These chambers either provided accommodation for the inhabitants, were used to store equipment or food, or were kitchens. In the course of our excavations, we observed two clear phases (II-III) marked by architectural changes and by the raising of floors. We also recovered evidence for a phase preceding the building of the fort, Phase IV, although it is doubtful that the site was fortified then.

In the north-eastern corner of the fort, we traced a 3mx6m surface built entirely of brick, apparently the platform for a set of wooden stairs that led to the top of the wall. In this corner of the fort the buttress-like projection no doubt served as a corner tower. The northern wing of the fort included a group of rooms and courtyards belonging to two major phases of construction (Phases II-III). A few circular refuse pits cut into the debris of Phase II imply that the western wing continued to be occupied for a while (Phase I) after the destruction of the fort in Phase II. A small courtyard adjacent to the enclosure wall apparently functioned as a kitchen; it contained seven taboons, each about 70 cm in diameter, which had been sunk into the floor. One of the rooms adjacent to the brick-floored platform contained a large Egyptian pithos, about 1 m in diameter and 1.5 m high, with a highly burnished surface. It belonged to the earliest phase of the fort, Phase III, and lay in a pit, that had been cut into the sterile sand. The upper part of the pithos had been chipped off in antiquity, perhaps during the construction of Phase II. Its shoulder is decorated with large cartouches which were deeply incised before the vessel was fired. Nearby were found the fragments of a second vessel that also had been incised with large cartouches (Pl. F; Fig. 7). Orly Goldwasser studied the fragmentary inscriptions and convincingly restored the names of

Merneptah's successor, Seti II (ca. 1216-1210 B.C.E.) (Goldwasser 1980:34). Fragments of a jar identical in type to ours and similarly incised with cartouches of Seti II were uncovered by Sir Flinders Petrie on the stone paved courtyard of the Governors Residency at Tell el-Far'ah, in the Besor basin (Starkey and Harding 1932: Pls. LXI,LXIV:74). The presence of these vessels, no doubt the property of the administration, in North Sinai and in southern Canaan bears testimony to the Egyptian administration of those areas.

The fort's western wing was very densely built, with clusters of rooms used as dwellings and for storage and long corridors and installations that opened into the center of the fort. The floors were made of brick material and beaten earth except for one room, in which the floor was paved with brick. In a number of rooms a single course of bricks laid on their narrow side was constructed against the wall; in all likelihood they supported benches or beds. Analysis of the fort's plan suggests that the western wing was used for dwelling, storage, and other domestic activities. The smaller rooms which were 12 sq m on the average, were dwellings, the larger rooms, some 25 sq m on the average, probably were used for public functions; the long narrow halls were repositories for equipment and for storage; additional storehouses with wide courtyards were built against the enclosure wall; and yet another group of clay taboons were built near one of the walls.

Building remains and floors of the later phase (Phase II) indicated extensive re-use of the original structures. A large part of the western wing is occupied by the well-preserved remains of a spacious structure, Building 500, That probably served some public function, perhaps as an administrative center. The structure was enclosed by a wall about 1 m wide and comprised a number of large rooms and a spacious courtyard. Building 500 was destroyed by fire, leaving in its destruction considerable heaps of bricks. In any event, judging by the many refuse pits and burials in the dwelling area, we suggest that, in Phase II the fort was in an advanced stage of disrepair and had already been partly abandoned. It is likely that sections of the enclosure wall had already collapsed and the gatehouse, through neglect, was no longer effective as a security feature. We may recall that in Phase II, the gateway had become the site of cooking and other activities. At a still later stage (Phase I), following the fort's destruction, the ruined sections were resettled; however that phase is very poorly documented in the archaeological record. It appears to have been settled by squatters who left behind a few refuse pits cut into the floor of Phase II. Finally, we also found evidence of a fourth stage, which preceded the building of the fort. It was represented by the skeleton of an adult, lying under the enclosure wall of the major phase, Phase III. The nature of the remains recorded in Phase IV and the fact that they cover only a limited area, suggests that, in its earliest phase of occupation, site A-289 had been occupied by a small settlement, perhaps an unfortified way station or even a temporary encampment.

Adult and child burials were recorded in various parts of the fort under floors and under the fallen brick debris: the skeleton of an adult male was discovered inside the northern buttresses of the gatehouse, and the skeleton of a child, the body oriented north, lying in the supine position, with its hands folded on its chest was recovered in the northern wing. The flexed burial of an adult lay nearby, its head similarly oriented to the north, but its face turned west. The extremely friable skeletal remains of infants were uncovered in several different areas within the fort. Although some of the adult and child skeletons do indeed belong to the phase of the original construction (Phase III), most are contemporary with the later period (Phase II), when the fort was no longer in full operation. The preliminary examination of the skeletal remains suggested that most of the skeletons are to be classed anthropometrically with those of the populations of North Sinai and southern Canaan.[16] This conclusion not only enhances our over-all understanding of the ethnic composition of northern Sinai, but defines in particular the population make-up of the Egyptian administered stations and forts in the area. It appears now that during the New Kingdom the population of North Sinai, the Shasu of the Egyptian record, was incorporated into the Egyptian military and civil administration on the "Ways of Horus". The burials we found of women, children, and infants in both major phases of A-298 bear witness to the fact that the forts in northern Sinai had not been manned by units of the Egyptian standing army, but rather by paramilitary or militia units recruited from the local population, whose families lived in the forts or in the nearby encampments. We must conclude therefore that in the New Kingdom, as later in the Assyrian and Persian periods, Egypt wove the local population into the fabric of her administration in North Sinai.[17]

The ceramic repertoire of Phase III comprised a relatively high percentage of vessels characteristic of southern Canaan toward the end of the Late Bronze Age. These included many shallow straightsided bowls with string cut bases, carinated kraters, large flasks decorated with concentric circles painted in red, and numerous storage jars with stump bases and a sharply carinated shoulder. The ceramic collection of Phase II was already represented by typical Early Iron Age classes, such as storage jars with a straight, tall neck and bowls with a cyma profile. A group of sherds of very late Philistine ware were recorded in the latest pits and on the surface of the site (Phase I). These finds indicate that in the eleventh, or possibly in the early tenth century B.C.E., a poor squatter's settlement or encampment existed near the fort and over its ruins. Furthermore, the ceramic repertoire of both Phases III and II is represented by a large number of locally made vessels modeled directly on Egyptian types, as well as by imported Egyptian products typical of the XIXth and XXth dynasties. Phase III is also represented by many sherds of imported Cypriote ware, such as dipper juglets of the White-Shaved family, milk bowls of White Slip ware, jugs and juglets of the Base Ring class, and Mycenaean stirrup vases, pyxides, and flasks. In the destruction debris of Building 500 of Phase II, we recovered a local copy of an Aegean bell-shaped bowl of Mycenaean IIIC ware, which dates to the early twelfth century B.C.E. In phases III and II, local versions of Aegean and Cypriote pottery types were recorded. The Haruba fort pottery collection is best paralleled in XIXth and XXth Dynasty deposits at Deir el-Medineh, Gurob and Tell el-Yehudiyeh in Lower Egypt, as well as at sites in the western Negev and the Gaza region, such as Tell Sera', Tell el-Far'ah, and Deir el-Balah (cf. Petrie 1891: Pls. XVII-XX; 1906: Pls. XXXIC-D; Brunton and Engelbach 1927: Pls. XXXIII-XXXIX; Nagel 1938: Dothan 1972: Castel 1980). Among the special finds, there was a group of scarabs, typical of the XIXth and XXth dynasties, clay duck heads that once decorated clay bowls, clay cobra heads — Egyptian uraei — a stone fitting from a chariot and fragments of a sandstone sphinx-like statuette (cf. Peet and Woolley 1923: Pl. XXIII:5; Rowe 1940: Pls. XLIIA:2,5,XLVA:4; James 1978: Pl. XI:b). This rich collection well represents the Late Bronze and Early Iron Ages, or the XIXth-XXth dynasty material culture and convincingly reflects the socio-political relationship between Egypt and Canaan in the late Empire period (Oren 1985:52-56).

The fort at Haruba is unique both in its excellent state of preservation and the rich collection of finds that enabled us to date its different settlement phases. Thanks to this discovery, it is now possible to reconstruct accurately the military architecture of the "Ways of Horus" and examine it against the representation of forts that are depicted in the reliefs in the Temple of Amun at Karnak. About twenty stations, of which eleven were fortified structures of different dimensions and plans, appear in the relief. Some of the forts are very small and have corner towers; others are considerably larger and much more complex in plan — they appear to have had a second story and perhaps also an inner citadel. The position of the entrance also varies from fort to fort. Scholarly debate over the reliability of the representations at Karnak revolves around how realistically the North Sinai forts are drawn (Badawy 1968:446-474; Naumann 1971:311-315). In the light of the new evidence from North Sinai it appears that the artist depended on a basic fort model that he altered at liberty. This conclusion finds support in contemporary Egyptian relief and wall paintings that portray military expeditions to Canaan (Yadin 1963:148-150, 205-217). In these representations, Canaan's fortified cities are remarkably identical to the forts that were planned and constructed by Egyptian architects in northern Sinai. The Egyptian artist evidently used the same model to render both the large, heavily fortified cities, such as Ashkelon in Canaan and Kadesh in Syria, and the small and medium-sized forts on the "Ways of Horus". It is not unlikely therefore, that the forts in the Karnak relief are stereotypes used to represent more or less along the same lines any military installation outside Egypt. Differences in a fort's size of plan would then reflect only the artist's desire to vary and enliven a scene, or the amount of space available in the composition. In sum, the archaeological evidence yielded by the Haruba fort in tandem with the remains from similarly fortified structures recorded elsewhere in northern Sinai, augments and complements the picture drawn by the written sources and the reliefs concerning the effectiveness of Egypts' military system in the "Way of Horus".

In the Haruba complex, but not far from the fort, our expedition explored an impressive site that has added significantly to our reconstruction of the Egyptian administration of the "Ways of Horus". The site, A-345 on the expedition map, is situated about 400 m north of the fort and near the coastline.

Site A-345 is located right in the middle of active coastal sand dunes; in fact, most of it is buried under the ridges of towering dunes, some of them more than 20 m high. The settlement's original boundaries are unknown, but judging from its building remains and pottery deposits, we may suspect that it once covered an area of more than 6 acres[18] (Oren 1980:32-33).

In the course of three seasons of excavations (1980-1982) our expedition explored about 1/2 acre on the site and identified three building units; a complex of magazines in the center of the site, a "casemate-walled" area in the north-west, and an industrial quarter on the east (Fig. 8). The plan is symmetrical, and the walls of the structures were carefully laid. The architectural and planning features are purely Egyptian: ground plan, building and bonding techniques, and the standard brick size. The magazine complex in the center of the site included a series of long halls that opened into a central courtyard, 20 m x 15 m in size. The courtyard was divided in the middle by a thin partition wall and was enclosed by another wall that was one brick brick thick. The halls in the magazine measured 10 m x 3 m and had brick floors. Their well-plastered walls were only one brick or 36 cm thick, and were preserved to a height of approximately 1 m. Heaps of fallen bricks and even complete sections of walls that belonged to the ruined superstructure lay within the magazines. The debris rested directly on a layer of sand that must have seeped in after the site was abandoned but definitely before the roof, followed by the walls, collapsed. The floor of the magazines was heaped with a thick layer of carbonized grain and similar deposits were noted in the courtyard in front of them, that had no doubt spilled from sacks of grain as they were loaded and unloaded.

A variety of rooms and small compartments lay to the east, south, and west of the magazines, many with brick-paved floors. They probably served as dwellings, offices, and archives. The openings to the rooms were usually flanked by symmetrically built brick buttresses with round corners, coated with a thick layer of plaster. The excavation focused on the last phase of occupation in A-345. In several places, however, both in the magazines and the courtyards, soundings under the floors yielded clear evidence of an earlier stratum that included building remains, domestic installations, and storage and refuse pits. Judging from the similarity in the pottery from the two phases and the absence both of a destruction layer or any evidence to indicate that the earlier site had been abandoned, we can assume that occupation was not interrupted and that the last phase of settlement represents a reorganization of the site on a much grander scale.

Excavations in the north-western wing brought to light a "casemate" structure, at least 25 m long, formed by thin, well-plastered walls. Plastered brick benches were built against the walls and the interior of the structure was partitioned by thin buttressed walls. The deposit of fallen brick material had accumulated to a height of 1.50 m. Our conclusion that the site was probably not fortified is supported by the fact that this thin-walled "casemate" structure forms its northern boundary.

One of the most important discoveries at A-345 is the industrial quarter, which included a potter's workshop. The industrial quarter, was separated from the rest of the settlement by a well-built, brick partition wall, no doubt to avoid contaminating the magazine and service area with the constant smoke and soot from the kilns. The location of the workshop at the eastern end of the site makes perfect sense: the prevailing winds in northern Sinai are north-west to south-east and would carry the polluted air away from the settlement. Our excavation made it possible to follow in detail all the methods and procedures employed in this workshop, including the preparation of the clay, the shaping of the vessels and their firing in the kilns. The discovery of a potter's workshop from the New Kingdom illuminated our understanding of the ceramic technology of this period in northern Sinai and, in fact, in Egypt as well.

The northern part of the industrial quarter was occupied by a complex of installations that served in all probability for storing the clay. The clay was prepared here in water reservoirs and finally softened under the potter's feet until its consistency became elastic and could be easily shaped on the potter's wheel. The many additions and rebuildings of these installations suggest that heavy use occasioned the frequent need for modifications or repairs. On the floors of these installations were registered clunks of clean, light-brown clay, closely resembling the kind used by local brick manufacturers. Adjacent to the storage installations, a complete potter's kiln was uncovered (Pl. G). It was preserved to a height of 1.50 m with an outer circumference of 1.80 m. Brick steps on the west site of the kiln gave the potter access to the upper chamber where the pots were fired. The lower or fuel chamber, was about 1 m high. It was dug into the sandy soil beneath the surface, a feature probably intended to aid in maintaining the heat withing the chamber. A southern orientation for the opening was no doubt chosen to avoid prevailing North Sinai northwesterly winds. In addition, the entrance to the kiln, measuring some 0.70 m across, was flanked by short walls that protected it further against the cooling drafts. Some sections of the brick floor of the upper chamber are preserved *in situ*, but the rest had caved into the fuel chamber. That fired brick floor, or grating, was pierced by a network of small holes, each about 0.10 m wide, designed to allow hot air into the firing chamber above. The grate was 0.20-25 m thick and covered on either side with a thick layer of plaster. It was supported in a somewhat unusual manner: it did not rest on a central column, rather its convex shape distributed its weight evenly down the walls. A careful examination of the fragments from the fuel chamber revealed that, in addition to the holes in the grating, a clay pipe had also been constructed in the wall of the kiln, terminating in an opening on the wall of the firing chamber. This device had helped both to control the temperature in the firing chamber, and to carry off the smoke from the

Pl. G — Potter's kiln. Site A-345

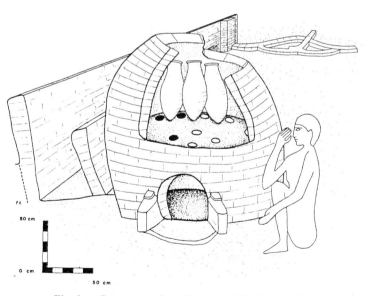

Fig. 9 — Reconstruction of potter's kiln, Site A-345

burning fuel. The upper, or firing, chamber is preserved to about 0.50 m above the grate: we estimate its original height to have been approximately 1 m and its inner diameter 1.40 m.

Judging from the shape of the walls of the firing chamber, the kiln was domed and completed with a wide opening for loading and unloading vessels and a chimney to control the temperature (Fig. 9). A series of layers of vitrified plaster bear witness to the multiple repairs and additions that the structure must have undergone. This type of kiln, with its separate fuel and firing chambers, represents an advanced stage of ceramic technology; the potter could exercise complete control over both the firing conditions and the temperature in the upper chamber. The entire kiln area was covered with refuse from the potter's workshop: taboon fragments, wastes, fired bricks, charcoal, and ash. One room to the west of the kiln contained large quantities of industrial waste, as well as many fragments of pottery stands with a tall, trumpet-shaped foot, including unfired specimens and chunks of unused clay. In another room nearby we recorded a group of especially large flower pots. The literally tons of pottery recovered in the industrial area are important for indexing typology in ceramic assemblages at Haruba.

A second potter's kiln, somewhat smaller, was unearthed in the southern wing of the site (Pl. H). It, too, is a round, brick structure, preserved to the height of approximately 1 m with well-plastered walls about 1 m in diameter. The fuel chamber is similar to that in the large kiln, though its opening faces west and widens, like a funnel, towards the interior of the structure. Thick clay tiles, which had once lined the floor of the fuel chamber were found in the bottom of the installation. The floor of the firing chamber was not preserved, but it appears to have been supported by brick "brackets", judging from the brick remains jutting out from the inside of the wall. Remains of sections from the kiln's wall indicate that the upper part was either conical or dome shaped, and that, as with the first kiln, a wide opening provided access to the firing chamber. On the eastern side of the kiln we found a small round structure filled with fallen bricks. In a modern Egyptian potter's workshop, a room adjacent to the kiln sometimes houses the potter's wheel, and it is not unlikely that our small structures served the same purpose. Alternatively, it may have been used to store the fuel for the kiln. Around the kiln were found large heaps of ash, charcoal, and other industrial waste.

A preliminary petrographic study of the pottery from Site A-345 demonstrated that most of the vessels had been produced of the same light or greenish-brown or buff-colored clay.[19] The remaining vessels were made either of Delta silt or of a clay with high lime content. By and large, the shapes represented in this assemblage are characteristically Egyptian. The Haruba potter evidently specialized in the production of certain specific types of pottery which were copied directly from the Egyptian ceramic repertoire — for instance, various types of bowls and kraters; the whole range of drop-shaped vessels; offering tables, consisting of tall stands on a high, trumpet-shaped base with a small bowl on top (Pl. I), and flower pots with heavy, frequently perforated bases bearing deep thumb indentations.

The evidence from Haruba suggests that the potter's workshop was under the auspices of the Egyptian administration and provided a specific line of vessels to other Egyptian sites in North Sinai. Here as in other sites in northern Sinai, the percentage of Canaanite vessels is small and limited to storage jars. Excavations have yielded fine examples of imported Cypriote wares (Pl. J) but, hardly any Mycenaean pottery. In sum, the corpus of pottery from site A-345 is typical of Egyptian sites from the XVIII Dynasty, and particularly in the 14th century B.C.E., e.g., el-Amarna and Malkata (Peet and Woolley 1923: Pls. XLVI-LIV; Frankfort and Pendlebury 1933: Pls. LI-LIV; Kemp 1981:16-19; Fig. 7).

The discovery of an intact potter's workshop dating to the

New Kingdom is of immense importance to the study of Egyptian pottery in northern Sinai and its affiliation to Egyptian ceramic technology because the site, architecturally and in terms of its ceramic repertoire, is Egyptian in every respect. Indeed, hardly any examples of a potter's workshop dating to the New Kingdom period have been found on Egyptian soil, with the result that construction methods and production processes are still not well understood.[20]

For other sources of analogy to Haruba, we must look at the well-decorated clay and wooden models from Egypt as well as at the vivid depictions in wall paintings of the period which are so invaluable in any attempt to reconstruct daily life in ancient Egypt. Unfortunately, the models are usually only schematic and lack pertinent details, and the wall paintings only provide the kiln's shape and outer appearance (Holthoer 1977:27-37). In spite of these limitations, we can construct an authentic picture of the Egyptian ceramic industry during the New Kingdom.

The potter's workshop was a favorite subject of Egyptian artists and was very frequently represented in wall paintings from the Old Kingdom on. The paintings and wooden models indicate that the Egyptians were familiar with different types of workshops and kilns. Simple kilns, in which one compartment took both the vessels and the fuel, and very developed types with separate firing and fuel chambers are depicted (Holthoer 1977:34-37, Fig. 49). The latter types, usually biconical or cylindrical in shape, allowed for more accurate control of the temperature and duration of the fire and of the amount of oxygen permitted to enter either compartment. The more advanced type included a grate and, as at Haruba, clay channels were built along the wall to ensure the even distribution of the heat. Oxygen was introduced into the fuel chamber through either the upper or lower openings, to regulate the intensity of the flames. The kilns at Haruba are evidently of the cylindrical type. The steps found near the larger installation suggest that its

Pl. H — Second potter's Kiln. Site A-345

Pl. I — Tall tubular stand offering
table, Site A-345

Pl. J — Cypriote base ring juglet,
Site A-345

height may have been about 2 m; however the smaller kiln was low enough not to require steps to the opening of the firing chamber. Neither Egyptian models nor wall paintings give us any clue about the size of the upper opening, but because it was the only means of access for loading and unloading vessels from the kiln, it must have been wide enough to allow the potter or his assistant to work without damaging the pots. It is also impossible for us to determine just from the wall paintings what the internal arrangements were for regulating the temperature in the upper chamber. From the clay channel and the fragments of a clay pipe found in the larger Haruba kiln we deduced that highly developed kilns included internal structural features for maintaining a steady and evenly distributed flow of heat in the upper chamber.

An extensive potter's quarter dating from the Late Bronze and Iron Ages that included the remains of no fewer than twenty kilns and related installations for preparing clay and finishing vessels was recently excavated at Sarepta on the Phoenician coast (Pritchard 1975:71-84; 1978:111-126). Unlike the kilns at Haruba, the firing chambers in the Sarepta kilns were usually built above ground level and contained a short projecting wall that supported the roof of the fuel chamber and helped to bear the weight of the vessels placed in the firing chamber above it. At Haruba, no such special support seemed necessary, either because the installation was relatively small or because the convex shape of the dividing grate performed the same function. At Sarepta a section of the plastered floor of the firing chamber, preserved *in situ*, was honeycombed in a manner similar to that of the grates at Haruba, but no particular attention was paid to the wind pattern in orienting the openings of the fuel chambers. Like the workshop at Haruba, that at Sarepta was in use for a long period of time and underwent many repairs and modifications. However, in the entire potter's workshop at Sarepta, not a single kiln was preserved with the remains of its upper chamber. The well preserved kiln at Haruba thus remains a rare example of its kind from the Bronze Age in this region.[21]

Recent discoveries in northeastern Sinai and the western Negeb complete our picture of the Egyptian administrative and military system in the coastal region of the northern Sinai that we have been drawing here. They further demonstrate the strong influence of Egyptian culture in this region. Excavations by the Ben Gurion University expedition at Tell Sera' (Biblical Ziklag), on the north bank of Nahal Gerar, have yielded settlement strata from the 14th-12th centuries B.C.E. that contained a great deal of Egyptian material. Of particular interest was a massive structure, built in the Egyptian style that was most probably the residence of the local Egyptian governor during the reign of Ramesses III (Oren 1985:39-45 and n.6 for bibliography). The destruction layer of this building included a group of bowls with inscriptions in Egyptian hieratic script describing administrative matters, specifically, large measures of grain that had been brought as a produce tax or tribute to the local governor or temple (Goldwasser 1984:77-93). These documents, coupled with the large collection of Egyptian objects — of clay, alabaster, faience, and glass — do make a strong case for this structure having been designed as an Egyptian administrative center. Tell Sera' and other sites in the western Negev, such as Tell el-Far'ah, Tell Jemmeh, and Tell el-'Ajjul, also have provided material evidence for the Egyptianization of southern Canaan (Oren 1985:46-50).

The Egyptian center recently explored at Deir el-Balah is additional testimony of the Egyptianization of the settlement in the region of Gaza. Excavations at Deir el-Balah uncovered sections of a cemetery with burials of men, women and children in anthropoid coffins (Dothan 1979). It is worth noting that although the skeletal remains are similar to New Kingdom burials in Lower Egypt, not a single skeleton at Deir el-Balah was of the Negroid type that characterizes Egyptian cemeteries (Dothan 1979:92-97). Deir el-Balah may have been the burial ground for officers and officials and their families in the local Egyptian administration in the Gaza region, as well as for Canaanites, also in the service of Egypt, who had adopted Egyptian burial customs.

The Hebrew University expedition to Deir el-Balah has also uncovered the impressive remains of the settlement that had no doubt been a fort and an administrative center on the eastern end of the "Ways of Horus" (Dothan 1981:126-131). The settlement strata dating to the 14th and 13th centuries B.C.E., included massive mud brick forts completed with corner buttresses or towers. Nearby, an artificial basin was excavated, 25 m x 25 m and about 5 m deep, that had served as reservoir for water. Remains of a similar reservoir, although constructed and lined differently, were found at Bir el-ʻAbd (cf. above). It seems that such reservoirs were common at Egyptian stations in northern Sinai and the Gaza Strip.[22]

The discovery of administrative centers alongside military installations adds another dimension to our understanding of Egypt's government in northern Sinai. It appears that, allied to the military system, a bureaucratic organization supervised commerce, collected duties and taxes, and met the needs of the soldiers, in the garrison and in the campaigning armies, who stopped there for provisions or to camp. When the military hold over the region weakened in the late XVIIIth Dynasty, many of those stations were deserted and some were never reoccupied. Later, in the course of the reconstruction of the system, it appears that some sites were relocated. We have seen, for example, that the fort at Haruba was built more than half a kilometer from the administrative center A-345. An analysis of ceramic collections from such XVIIIth Dynasty sites as Bir el-ʻAbd and A-345 has shown that the ratio of Egyptian to Canaanite pottery is drastically different from sites of the XIXth and XXth Dynasty. In the former group there are few Canaanite objects, whereas in the latter the bulk of the material is Canaanite. The ratios are an important index of the degree of cultural interaction between Canaan and the Egyptian Delta in the land bridge of North Sinai. The abundance of Canaanite finds in XIXth and XXth Dynasty sites no doubt reflects the ever-growing involvement of Egypt in Canaan, which is also evident in the increasing "Canaanization" of the Egyptian Delta.[23]

The excavations at North Sinai sites demonstrated their close relationship in terms of architecture and material culture to New Kingdom Egypt. The building techniques, ground plans and over-all schemes have identical parallels in several major Egyptian sites, such as el-Amarna, Gurob and Malkata in western Thebes. These similarities suggest, for instance, that site A-345 may have been an Egyptian administrative center in North Sinai. The administrative complexes at el-Amarna and Malkata as at Haruba, were equipped with clusters of magazines for storing the grain supply (most likely collected as taxes). The architectural units at el-Amarna were similarly surrounded by thin enclosure walls and were composed of long halled magazines which were arranged in rows and opened into spacious courtyards. The associated units served as dwellings, offices, and archives as well as granaries (Frankfort and Pendlebury 1933: Pls. V-XV, esp. XIII-XV). An interesting parallel of Egyptian architecture on the edge of the eastern Delta (the western terminus of the "Ways of Horus") was explored in 1917 by Cledat at Jebel Hassa, between the Bitter Lake and the city of Suez (Cledat 1919:209). The Jebel Hassa structure consisted of three long halls, one of which contained a chapel dedicated to Hathor and Suteh, the two deities usually identified by the Egyptians with the East. The entrance to this structure was through a small opening flanked by massive buttresses, each some 2 m wide, a feature suggesting to Cledat the fortlike structure (Migdol?) in the Karnak relief. However, the size of the building, and its thin outer wall indicate that it was not fortified. Large pottery containers for grain were embedded in the floors of the long halls, and many fragments of New Kingdom reliefs, in particular from the time of Seti I and Ramesses II, were registered in those compartments. It is noteworthy that the method of building internal partitions and the extensive use of inner buttresses at Jebel Hassa are comparable to those at site A-345 and, like at the Haruba fort (A-289), Cledat recorded burials under the floors.

The new evidence bearing on the later phases of Egypt's presence on the "Ways of Horus" indicate that Egypt dominated the region for much longer than was once thought. Of course it is doubtful that the Egyptian network in northern Sinai functioned optimally during the XXth Dynasty given the condition we found at the Haruba fort of loosened controls and lessened activity. Building 500 of the fort probably served as the administrative center of this period; yet other parts of the fort were already occupied by pits and burials and the main gateway was blocked, suggesting that the site had been partially abandoned. The finds from northern Sinai now complement those from Canaan proper and confirm the evidence from Egyptian documents of the late Ramesside dynasty concerning Egypt's control of the major highways in Canaan as well as the mines in Southern Sinai and the Arabah (Oren 1985:52-56).

The finds from the North Sinai survey are of considerable importance in reconstructing the history of Egypt's administrative and military system in North Sinai. These finds complement the picture derived from Egyptian documents such as Papyrus Anastasi V and VI of the late XIX Dynasty concerning Egypt's control over the "Ways of Horus" (Wilson 1955:259). It is now evident that Egypt's major fortification system was built in the XIXth Dynasty — the period commemorated by the Karnak reliefs for the restoration of Egypt's military system along the "Ways of Horus" under Seti I. The large pottery containers at Haruba fort inscribed with the names of Seti II, which no doubt were the property of the

Egyptian administration, provide evidence of Egyptian control in Canaan and Sinai toward the end of the XIXth Dynasty. It has long been argued that in the period of total anarchy between the death of Merneptah and the ascent of Ramesses III, Egypt lost its important position in the international arena and its hold over Canaan (cf. above). Yet, the new evidence from northern Sinai and complementary evidence from the turquoise and copper mines in southern Sinai, and in the Arabah, and from sites in the western Negeb and the Jordan valley clearly show that Egypt still maintained a firm hold over the "Ways of Horus" and a strong presence in Canaan under Seti II and his widow and successor, Queen Twosret.[24]

A comparative study of Egypt's military and administrative organization in border areas of the empire particularly on the Nubian frontier, may aid considerably in the reconstruction of Egypt's policy along the "Ways of Horus" as well. The similarity of the military architecture in Nubia to that of northern Sinai is extremely revealing. Dozens of sites that served as staging posts, commercial stations, military forts or garrisons, and administrative and cult centers have been recorded along the Nubian frontier (Blackman 1937; Emery 1965:172-207; Kemp 1972:651-656; Clarke 1916:155-179). The literary record also provides welcome evidence of common organizational procedures at border-crossing points. For example, a border report from Semna on the second cataract in Nubia, although of an earlier period (the reign of Amenemhat III), clearly details a picture similar to that of Papyrus Anastasi VI (Smither 1945:1-10). The border crossings were guarded by special police recruited from the local Nubian tribes, like the desert police force on the "Ways of Horus" recorded in Papyrus Anastasi V (Wilson 1955:259). No doubt these soldiers were also natives of the region.

Likewise, a study of the settlement pattern and administrative system along the Mediterranean coast of the western desert between Alexandria and the Libyan border might reveal interesting points of similarity to the "Ways of Horus"; their topography is so similar that Egypt's economic and military interests in both areas may also have been comparable. Regrettably, our knowledge of the history and archaeology of Egypt's western frontier is very limited. Sporadic exploration along the coast of the Mediterranean between Alexandria and el-Alamein, revealed the remains of settlement sites with architecture not dissimilar to that of North Sinai, that may have been a chain of fortified stations, caravanserai, and wells along the major road to Libya.[25] This system of garrisons and stations was apparently intended to prevent the Libyan Berber pastoralists from infiltrating into the Western Delta and probably also to encounter the challenge of an attack by Libyan tribes who had banded together with groups of the Sea-Peoples. It is no wonder, then that the kings of the XIX and XXth dynasties established a complex military organization between the western Delta and the Libyan border that probably did not differ much from the one on the eastern frontier. It is significant, however, that although from a military point of view the problems posed by both regions may have been similar, the eastern border was far more vital because it linked Egypt to its Asian provinces. After all, the royal residence of the Ramesside kings was built near the western end of the "Ways of Horus" precisely because the location offered the best strategic advantages for the daily supervision of operations in their Asiatic province. The importance which Egypt attached to the eastern border is reflected in the documents dealing with Egyptian military campaigns to Asia, the reports from the border garrison of Sile and by the central position occupied by the "Ways of Horus" in the relief at the Temple of Amun at Karnak.

NOTES

1 Gardiner 1920:99-116. The biblical phrase "Way of the land of the Philistines" (Ex. 13:17) was taken by some authorities actually as the proper name of the southern section of the coastal highway, see, for instance, Aharoni 1967:42.

2 For summary and bibliography see Oren 1985:52-56, 1985a:223-226.

3 The New Kingdom frontier garrison Sile has long been identified with Tell Abu-Seifeh, east of Qantara. It is worth noting that a surface survey and soundings in 1972 that were conducted by the present writer on behalf of Ben Gurion University at Tell Abu-Seifeh yielded a large collection of pottery. Except for a few specimens of the Saite period, none of the sherds is earlier than the Persian period. The third station, "Migdol of Seti", has been traditionally equated with the same locality mentioned in Exodus 14:9 and Numbers 33:7 and identified with Tell el-Ḥêr, south of Pelusium. This identification depends largely on documents of the Classical period, in particular on the Antonine Itinerary, which indicates a station named Magdolum, midway between Pelusium and Sile. A re-evaluation of the textual references against the new archaeological evidence makes such an identification most unlikely, see Oren 1984:33-35. For Gaza see Katzenstein 1982:111-113.

4 For instance, the fort of the fifth station and the well of the seventh were both named Seti Merneptah. The name of the eighth station is the "well of Men-Maat-Re" and the "Well of Matok" (perhaps the "sweet well"?). The ninth station is simply called "the city which his majesty built and in the Well of Ḥbrt", see Gardiner 1920:113.

5 For past explorations in this region see detailed bibliography in Oren 1973:198, n. 2. Also see excavations in 1935-36 at Tell Abu-Salima near Sheikh Zuweid, Petrie and Ellis 1937.

6 The survey of northern Sinai was carried out, under the direction of the present writer, on behalf of the Archaeology Division, Ben Gurion University of the Negev. The Southern Command of the IDF was most helpful in the logistic needs of the expedition. The expedition was aided in every way by A. Goren and B. Saas, Archaeological Liaison officers for Sinai, and D. Meiron, Archaeological Liaison officers for the Gaza region. The Israel Academy for Sciences made available a generous research grant for 1974-1975 seasons in Sinai.

   The writer is much indebted to the above named as well as the archaeological team of Ben Gurion University and students and volunteers who participated in the survey and excavations under most difficult conditions.

7   In some areas — for instance at Salamaneh, Mispaq and el-Mazar — the line of sites shifted north or south, most likely to avoid marshes or impassable ridges of active sand dunes that evidently existed at that time.

8   The majority of New Kingdom sites were located south of the Bardawil Lagoon. With the exception of Tell Riddan, near Khan Yunis, no New Kingdom sites were recorded directly on the coast of North Sinai. It seems that transport ships avoided the coast of Sinai altogether on their eastward journeys. Indeed the records from the Classical period emphasized how impossible it was for large vessels to land in the shallow waters off the Sinai Coast. Coastal sites were probably reached only by small boats and rafts that moved back and forth between the coast and the large ships anchored farther out at sea. Incidentally, it was in this manner that Pompeius landed on the shores of Cassion, where he met his tragic death.

It is most likely that the shallow inlet of the Haruba anchorage, which is used today by fishing boats in search of shelter, also functioned in antiquity as anchorage for unloading the stores and equipment brought to shore in small craft. Archaeological evidence of the use of such small boats was found near the Bardawil Lagoon in 1975 by a fisherman who caught a clay model of a boat in his net. A similar model of characteristic New Kingdom type was acquired by the Israel Museum and was reported to have been found near Gaza (perhaps at Deir el-Balah?) (see Basch 1976: Figs. 1-2, Pl. I:1-2). Evidence of a small anchorage, or a protected lee, and a stone quay was recorded recently near Tell Riddan. The site was scattered with stone anchors of the same type recorded at Kition in Cyprus, see Raban and Galili 1985:329-332. For the stone anchors see Frost 1970:16-19.

9   For a preliminary report see Oren 1973a:101-103; 1973b:112-113. Area supervisors in 1972 season were B. Saas, C. Clamer and F. Hawkin, and J. Baumgarten in 1973 season. Kibbutz Nahal-Yam kindly extended warm hospitality to the expedition.

10 See Badawy 1968:128-131; Peet and Woolley 1923: Pl. VII:2; Frankfort and Pendlebury 1933: Pl. XXVI: I; Kemp 1983: Pl. IV:2. It is noteworthy that grain silos usually stood in rows and not in clusters.

11 For figures on the distribution and size of the rations received by soldiers on campaign see, for example, Papyrus Anastasi I. The daily ration of an Egyptian battalion, according to this document, included 120 sheep; 1800 loaves of coarse bread, or one third of a loaf per soldier; 300 loaves of fine bread, or one sixteenth of a loaf per soldier; and 30 measures of wine, or one hundred and sixty-sixth of a measure for each Egyptian soldier. In I Samuel 25:18, there is a similar list recording the rations received by David's army. Interestingly, there is not a great deal of difference in the amounts of meat and bread; the Israelite soldiers received only half as

much wine as their Egyptian counterparts (!). For discussion see Malamat 1964:342-349.

12 The purpose of these vessels is not clear. They may have been used for planting or for measuring grain or even as bread molds. See Nagel 1938:192-193, Pls. XIII-XIV.

13 For a preliminary report see Oren 1980:26-33. S. Kornberg supervised the excavation of Site A-345 and R. Feinstein supervised Site A-289. M. Heiman, I. Eldar, M. Khalaila, M. Paran and Y. Yizarski were area supervisors in both sites. P. Louppen and P. Kaminski served as surveyors and S. Yadid as expedition administrator. The author expresses his gratitude to members of the team for their unfailing efforts and dedication under the most difficult conditions. The author is most grateful to Moshav Haruvit for the hospitality and co-operation during the survey and excavations in the region of Haruba.

14 The magnitude of this project is impressive: we have calculated that the enclosure wall and gatehouse alone contained 50,000 sq m of brick (figuring 65 bricks per square meter), not to mention the tens of thousands of bricks needed for the buildings within the walled area.

15 For discussion and bibliography see Oren 1984:10-13, also Spencer 1979a:132-137.

16 The author is grateful to Prof. B. Arensburg, Tel Aviv University, for this information.

17 For Sinai during the Assyrian and Persian periods see E.D. Oren, "North Sinai Before the Classical Period-History and Archaeology," in *The Sinai Peninsula*, Tel Aviv (forthcoming), also Eph'al 1982:74ff.

18 The remains of a double brick wall projecting from the western face of the sand dune, approximately 150 m from the edge of the excavated area, makes it very likely that the settlement was even larger.

19 Information kindly supplied by Mr. J. Glass.

20 So far the remains of kilns in Egypt date mainly from the Old and the Middle Kingdoms see Holthoer 1977:16-18; Leclant 1984: Figs. 33-34. A kiln that dates from the Persian period, 5th-4th century B.C.E. was recently discovered in East Karnak by a University of Toronto expedition. In this installation, as at Haruba, the opening to the fuel chamber is also opposite the prevailing winds (Redford 1978: Fig. 1).

21 See Petrie 1931: Pls. VI, LIV for Late Bronze Age kilns at Tell el-Ajjul.

22 The carved blocks, which bore cartouches with the names of Ramesses II, that were discovered south of Gaza may have belonged to a lintel of an Egyptian building, perhaps one of the easternmost forts on the "Ways of Horus." See Giveon 1975' 247-249. Similar blocks carved with Egyptian names of the XIXth and XXth dynasties have been recorded at Beth-Shean, Ashdod and Jaffa, see Weinstein 1981.

23 Compare, for example, the ratios of Egyptian to Canaanite Ceramic in

Early Bronze Age sites in North Sinai, Oren 1973:201.

24   Cf. above. The famous "Israel Stela" of Merneptah may suggest that, after all, this Pharaoh led a campaign to Canaan in his fifth year and reasserted Egypt's domination over the "Ways of Horus" and ·Canaan. See most recently Stager 1985:56*-64*.

25   Rowe 1954:484-500. According to Habachi (1984) the station and forts were built at intervals of about 50 km. It appears that the main building period along the West Coast occurred during the reign of Ramesses II. For recent explorations at Marsa Matruh see White 1985:3-17, esp. 10-17.

REFERENCES

Aharoni, Y., 1967. *The Land of the Bible: A Historical Geography*, London.

Astrom, P., 1972. *The Swedish Cyprus Expedition* Vol. IV, pt. 1c *The Late Cypriote Bronze Age, Architecture and Pottery*, Lund.

Badawy, A., 1968. *A History of Egyptian Architecture, The Empire or New Kingdom*, Los Angeles.

Basch, L., 1976. "Boat Models from the Near East", *Sephunim* 5:9-12 (Hebrew).

Blackman, H.M., "Preliminary Report on the Excavations at Sesebi: Northern Province, Anglo-Egyptian Sudan 1936-1937", *JEA* 23:145-151.

Brunton, G., and Engelbach, R., 1927. *Gurob* (British School of Archaeology in Egypt, Egyptian Research Account Twenty-fourth year, 1918), London.

Castel, G., 1980. *Deir el-Medineh 1970* (Fascicule I: Gournet Mar'el Nord), *Fouilles de l'Institute Francais d'Archeologie Orientale*, Tome XII/I, Caire.

Clarke, S., 1916. "Ancient Egyptian Frontier Fortresses", *JEA* III: 155-179.

Cledat, J., 1919. *BIFAO* XVI:201-228.

Dothan, T., 1972. "Excavations at the Cemetery of Deir el-Balah", *Qedem* (Monographs of the Institute of Archaeology, the Hebrew University of Jerusalem). 10. Jerusalem.

Dothan, T., 1981. "Notes and News: Deir el-Balah 1979-1980", *IEJ* 31:126-131.

Emery, W.B., 1965. *Egypt in Nubia*, London.

Eph'al, I., 1982. *The Ancient Arabs*, Jerusalem.

Faulkner, R.O., 1947. "The Wars of Setos I", *JEA*, 33:34-40.

Faulkner, R.O., 1975. In *Cambridge Ancient History* (3rd ed.), Ed. I.E.S. Edwards *et al.*, Vol. II, Pt. 2. Cambridge.

Frankfort, and Pendlebury, J.D.S., 1933. *The City of Akhenaten*, Pt. II, London.

Frost, H., 1970. "Some Cypriote Stone Anchors from Land Sites and From the Sea", *Report of the Department of Antiquities Cyprus*: 14-24.

Gardiner, A., 1920. "The Ancient Military Road Between Egypt and Palestine", *JEA* 6:99-116.

Goldwasser, O., 1980. "An Egyptian Store-Jar from Haruvit", *Qadmoniot* XIII:1-2:34 (Hebrew).

Goldwasser, O., 1984. "Hieratic Inscriptions from Tel Sera' in Southern Canaan", *Tel Aviv* 11:1:77-93.

Habachi, L., 1984. "Certain Sites To Be Examined Before It Is Too Late", *JSSEA* XIV:I.

Hayes, W.C., 1959. *The Scepter of Egypt*. Pt. II: *The Hyksos Period and the New Kingdom* (1675-1080 B.C.). New York.

Holthoer, R., 1977. *New Kingdom Pharaonic Sites: The Pottery*, Uppsala (The Scandinavian Joint Expedition to Sudanese Nubia, Vol. 5:I).

James, F., 1978. "Chariot Fittings from Late Bronze Age Beth Shan", *Archaeology in the Levant* (Essays for Kathleen Kenyon), ed. R. Moorey and P. Parr, Warminster, 102-115.

Kemp, B.J., 1972. "Fortified Towns in Nubia" in *Man, Settlement and Urbanism*, ed. P.J. Ucko *et al.*, London.

Kemp, B.J., 1981. "El Amarna, 1980", *JEA* 67.

Kemp, B.J., 1983. "Preliminary Report on the El-Amarna Expedition 1981-2", *JEA* 69.

Katzenstein, H.J., 1982. "Gaza in Egyptian Texts of the New Kingdom", *JAOS* 102:111-113.

Kitchen, K.A., 1982. *Pharaoh Triumphant: The Life and Times of Ramesses II*, Mississauga.

Leclant, J., 1984. *Orientalia* 53.

Malamat, A., 1964. "Military Rationing in Papyrus Anastasi I and the Bible", *The Military History of the Land of Israel in Biblical Times*, ed. J. Liver, Jerusalem: 342-349 (Hebrew).

Nagel, G., 1938. *La Céramique du Nouvel Empire A Deir el-Medineh*, Vol. I, Caire.

Naumann, R., 1971. *Architektur Kleinasiens*, Tübingen.

Oren, E.D., 1973. "The Overland Route Between Egypt and Canaan in the Early Bronze Age", *IEJ* 23:198-205.

Oren, E.D., 1973a. "An Egyptian Fortress on the Military Road between Egypt and Canaan", *Qadmoniot* 6:101-103 (Hebrew).

Oren, E.D., 1973b. "Notes and News: Bir el-'Abd (Northern Sinai)", *IEJ* 23:112-113.

Oren, E.D., 1980. "Egyptian New Kingdom Sites in Northern Sinai", *Qadmoniot* 13:26-33 (Hebrew).

Oren, E.D., 1984. "Migdol: A New Fortress on the Edge of the Eastern Nile Delta", *BASOR* 256:7-44.

Oren, E.D., 1985. "Governors Residencies in Canaan under the New Kingdom: A Case Study of Egyptian Administration", *JSSEA* XIV:2.

Oren, E.D., 1985a. in *Biblical Archaeology Today*, ed. J. Aviram, Jerusalem.

Peet, T.E., and Woolley, C.L. *The City of Akhenaten*, Pt. I, London.

Petrie, W.M.F., 1891. *Illahun, Kahun and Gurob*, London.

Petrie, W.M.F., 1906. *Hyksos and Israelite Cities* (British school of Archaeology in Egypt, and Egyptian Research Account Twelfth year, 1906), London.

Petrie, W.M.F., 1931. *Ancient Gaza*, I, London.

Petrie, F., and Ellis, J.C., 1937. *Anthedon (Sinai)*, London.

Pritchard, J.B. 1975. *Sarepta, A Preliminary Report on the Iron Age*, Philadelphia.

Pritchard, J.B., 1978. *Recovering Sarepta, A Phoenician City*, Princeton.

Raban, A., and Galili, E., 1985. "Recent Maritime Archaeological Research in Israel — A Preliminary Report", *The International Journal of Nautical Archaeology and Underwater Exploration*, 14:4:321-356.

Redford, D., 1978. "Son of the Sun-Disc", *ROM, Archaeological Newsletter* (New Series) 154.

Rothenberg, B., 1972. *Timna: Valley of the Biblical Copper Mines*, London.

Rowe, A., 1940. *The Four Canaanite Temples of Beth-Shan*, Pt. I (The Temples and Cult objects), Philadelphia.

Rowe, A., 1954. "A Contribution to the Archaeology of the Northern Desert, II", *Bull. John Rylands Library, Manchester*, 36.

Shea, W.H., 1977. "A Date for the Recently Discovered Eastern Canal of Egypt", *BASOR* 226:31-38.

Smither, P.C., 1945. "The Semnah Despatches", *JEA,* 31:3-10

Sneh, A., and Weissbrod, T., 1973. "Nile Delta: The Defunct Pelusiac Branch Identified", *Science* 180:59-61.

Sneh, A., *et al.*, 1977. "Evidence for an Ancient Egyptian Frontier Canal", *American Scientist* 63:542-548.

Spencer, A.J., 1979. *Brick Architecture in Ancient Egypt,* Warminster.

Spencer, A.J., 1979a. in *Glimpses of Ancient Egypt: Studies in Honour of H.W. Fairman* (ed. J. Ruffle), Warminster: 132-137.

Stager, L.E., 1985. "Marneptah, Israel and Sea Peoples: New Light on an Old Relief", *Eretz Israel* 18 (N. Avigad Volume), Jerusalem.

Starky, J.L., and Harding, L., 1932. *Beth Pelet II and Beth Pelet Cemetery*, London.

Weinstein, J.M., 1981. "The Egyptian Empire in Palestine — A Reassessment", *BASOR* 241:18-21.

White, D., 1985. "Excavations at Mersa Matruh, Summer 1985 *ARCE Newsletter* 131.

Wilson, J.A., 1955 in *Ancient Near Eastern Texts Relating to the Old Testament*, ed. J.B., Pritchard, Princeton.

Yadin, Y., 1963. *The Art of Warfare in Bible Lands*, Ramat Gan (Hebrew).

6

The Impact of Egypt on Canaan during the 18th and 19th Dynasties in the Light of the Excavations at Deir el-Balaḥ

Trude Dothan

INTRODUCTION

T HE route leading across the northern Sinai from the Egyptian Delta to Canaan was of vital importance throughout the rise and decline of the Egyptian empire. The highway had likely been established early in the 18th Dynasty since Tuthmosis III was able to travel with his army from Sile (Qantara) to Gaza, a distance of some 250 kms, in a mere ten days, indicating the existence of a well-maintained and guarded highway (ANET: 235).

Between 1972 and 1982 excavations were conducted under the auspices of the Hebrew University of Jerusalem and the Israel Exploration Society at a site near modern Deir el-Balaḥ, just south of Gaza, the Egyptian capital of Canaan during the New Kingdom.[1] This site, whose ancient identification remains unknown, was founded by Egypt in the 14th century and functioned both as an economic and administrative center and as a military outpost during different phases of its existence.

Hence, it serves as a "type-site" for Egyptian activity on the border of Canaan between the 18th and 20th Dynasties and for resultant Egypto-Canaanite relations.

At Deir el-Balaḥ the excavation team uncovered nine phases of settlement, with minor subdivisions, dating from the Late Bronze Age II through the Byzantine era (Dothan, T. 1981b). This article will examine the first three major phases at the site in the light of Egypto-Canaanite relations.

(1) Stratum IX — the founding of the site as an administrative settlement during the 18th Dynasty (the Amarna Age);

(2) Stratum VII — the existence of the site as a military outpost during the early 19th Dynasty;

(3) Strata VI-IV — renewed settlement at the site and its adjacent cemetery from the mid-19th Dynasty.

The last three phases at the site, Strata III-I, represent Philistine, Israelite, and Byzantine occupation levels. The Iron Age occupation at Deir el-Balaḥ, with its denouement of Egyptian presence and advent of Philistines and Israelites, reflects the larger picture of Canaan on the whole, with the sweep of many ethnic groups who overlapped and succeeded one another, in general maintaining their distinctive material cultural identities but inevitably assimilating some influences from their predecessors and contemporaries. The final phase at the site dates to the Byzantine period when massive movements of sand buried the site under the dunes. This shift in the topographical nature of the site was due to natural causes and not to the decline of agriculture, as previously thought.[2] The geological evidence from Deir el-Balaḥ for the transformation of a rich, arable area into a wasteland of sand provides important verification of the historical record of such ancient writers as Procopious of Gaza, who noted a similar phenomenon at the nearby site of Ḥalutza.[3]

The modern site is situated in the midst of towering sand dunes. As a result, only about one half acre of the settlement itself was excavated. The excavations, therefore, provide at most a window on the history of occupation at the site and not a complete picture. Surveys and trial digs conducted by the excavation team at selected locations in the surrounding area indicate that the ancient settlement spread in all directions; its precise perimeters remain undefined. In each occupation phase, then, only a segment of an area much larger than that excavated is seen.

STRATUM IX

Stratum IX, the earliest phase of the settlement, founded on virgin soil, was dated by the excavators to the Amarna era. This troubled time in Egyptian history witnessed a change in religious focus under Pharaoh Akhenaten that brought about far-reaching political, social, and economic ramifications. Historians have generally agreed that the era was marked by a focus on domestic activity and an ambivalence toward foreign policy reflective of the introspective nature of the king himself (Aldred 1971, Breasted 1948). The returen to a vigorous military policy occurred only under the successors of Akhenaten beginning with Horemheb.

However, systematic re-evaluation of the literary and archaeological data has been underway since the mid-1960s. The cumulative impact of this research increasingly points to a modicum of activity on both the eastern and southern borders of Egypt during Akhenaten's reign. Two main types of activity have been observed during this period in relation to Egypt's holdings in Canaan and Nubia: (1) preparations for, or the execution of, military campaigns and (2) building activity.

Three major sources provide evidence for the maintenance of an active military policy during the Amarna era: (1) the Amarna letters, (2) fragments of Amarna art depicting battle scenes, and (3) a series of historical stelae. The careful rereading by H. Reviv of the Amarna letters from the years of Akhenaten's rule has made clear that while Egyptian control of Canaan during this period appears to have remained stable, the Hittite threat on the border of Syria was strong. This necessitated preparations on the part of the Egyptian government for a military campaign including the gathering of provisions and the mustering of troops by the local Canaanite governors (Reviv 1966). Although the campaign during Akhenaten's reign does not seem to have materialized, such a military excursion to regain lost border holdings led by Horemheb during the reign of Tutankhamun is mentioned in an inscription in the Memphite tomb of Horemheb (Weinstein 1982). In addition, fragments of Amarna art from the Aton shrine at Karnak provide pictorial evidence for a battle against Asians (Schulman 1978; Several 1972; Redford 1979).

Activity on the Nubian front has been verified from depictions in Amarna tombs of battle scenes against Nubians and of bound Nubian prisoners-of-war and, most recently, from a series of commemorative stelae (from Buhen and Amada) recounting a campaign undertaken there in Akhenaten's twelfth regnal year (Schulman 1982).

Significant evidence for building activities on both Egyptian borders has been provided from archaeological excavations and surveys both past and present. Along the northern Sinai coast, two significant complexes were founded during the 14th century. Bir el-'Abd, located midway between the Suez Canal and Gaza, contained a water installation for irrigation and drinking supplies and an extremely well-preserved granary consisting of four cylindrical mud-brick silos (Oren 1973). Haruvit, in northeastern Sinai, contained storerooms, a courtyard, and a potter's workshop. It was abandoned without destruction at the end of the 14th century and not resettled (Oren 1983).

At Sesebi on the border of Nubia a walled fortress-town was constructed during the Amarna Age before Akhenaten's sixth regnal year, since depictions of the king found there are in the ordinary style of the 18th Dynasty and not in that of Tell el-Amarna. The rich material finds from this site, both in pottery (especially in Mycenaean imports) and in art objects, have close parallels to those from Amarna proper (Blackman 1937). The site, which may have had some slight Egyptian occupation early in the 18th Dynasty before its fortification under Akhenaten, flourished throughout the 19th Dynasty as well.

The evidence of the building and military activity during the Amarna Age are highly significant and provide a vivid backdrop against which to view the nature of the settlement founded at Deir el-Balaḥ.

The major architectural feature from Stratum IX was a large residence built around a man-made pond, similar in design to building complexes of the Amarna period in Egypt. This residence was composed of three mud-brick buildings set at a right angle. The two north-south buildings together measure approximately 50 m in length and contain the remains of as many as fifteen rooms. The single east-west building measures approximately 20 m in length and contains at least four to five rooms. The buildings border the pond on its eastern and southern perimeters. It is probable that these buildings are part of a larger settlement, although the northernmost and westernmost boundaries of the complex are as yet undetermined since they continue under the sand dunes.

The large crater-pond is square, measuring approximately 20 m x 20 m. The boundaries of the crater were traced and partially defined on all four sides. The quarried sides slope steeply into the virgin marl to a depth of 5 m. Both archaeological observation and geological investigation confirm that the crater is man-made. Since many of the mud bricks from the buildings had been formed from the same marl as the crater, it seems that the crater served as a quarry, at least in its initial phase. After the marl had been quarried, the crater served as a water reservoir (both in St. IX and throughout St. VII). The usage of the crater as a pond or reservoir is confirmed on the one hand by hydrological investigation and on the other by the known building pattern of the Amarna Age, evident in the residences excavated at Tell el-Amarna, in which building complexes were designed adjacent to a pond or lake (Petrie 1894; Ricke 1932; Ricke and Borchardt 1980).

A number of special finds from in and around the residence have close links to Tell el-Amarna proper. In one room of the residence, which had a well-preserved beaten earth floor, four worked stone *kurkar* bases were found. Measuring 13 cm x 13 cm, with sloping sides and a slight depression on top, they likely served as supports for the four legs of a bedstead. Although many well-known and well-preserved wooden beds have been found in Egypt, the only other stone bases known are from Tell el-Amarna, where an identical set was found in a bedroom niche.

Just to the west of the residence, in the open area alongside the building, a *favissa* (pit) was excavated which contained a clay bulla (seal) bearing four hieroglyphs, two *udjats* and two *nefers*. The closest parallel to this seal again comes from Tell el-Amarna and provides a good chronological indication of the date of the locus and the buildings of Stratum IX. This seal also significantly indicates possible correspondence between Tell el-Amarna proper and Deir el-Balaḥ, since bullae were used to seal papyrus letters.

Another room within the residence yielded about ten cylindrical pieces of jaspar (carnelian?) and blue frit scattered about on the floor. Traces of gold dotted the blue frit. Each cylinder was pierced through by a square aperture. Both the size of the pieces and the nature of the aperture indicated that they were not beads for a necklace. Rather, they should be reconstructed as a staff or flail, similar to the ones found in the tomb of Tutankhamun, with pieces of blue frit alternating with carnelian, mounted on a wooden rod which has long since deteriorated. The size and beauty of the objects give additional

proof of the specifically Egyptian character and high culture linking this stratum with the Amarna Age. Additionally, it is interesting to note that the parallel flail from the tomb of Tutankhamun has links of the same dimensions and bears a cartouche reading "Tutankhaten," not "Tutankhamun," indicating that the parallel flail was crafted early in Tutankhamun's life.

A number of rooms had well-preserved beaten earth floors upon which were large amounts of locally made pottery of Egyptian and Canaanite types, with the Egyptian types predominating. Among the Egyptian vessels, those painted with blue paint, the so-called "Amarna blue", were found. Some of the Egyptian vessels, such as a chalice and a small drop-shaped painted vessel, have exact parallels at Amarna proper.

In addition, a bronze razor-knife was recovered from the floor of the Armana residence, again with an exact parallel from Tell el-Amarna.

Although the cemetery associated with this phase of the settlement's existence was not located by our team, material relevant to Stratum IX has surfaced in private collections including coffins, a number of scarabs, alabaster vessels strongly reminiscent of those crafted during the Amarna era, and Aegean pottery types.

The cumulative evidence of the military activity in Canaan and Nubia during the Amarna Age and the building activity at sites such as Bir el-'Abd, Haruvit, and Deir el-Balaḥ are highly significant. Rather than Akhenaten's reign being a period of inactivity in foreign affairs, this era was characterized by continued Egyptian commitment and involvement in maintaining the strength of its borders and the stability of the empire. In light of this, the nature of the settlement founded at Deir el-Balaḥ during the Amarna era is extremely intriguing. The site is located on the furthest border of Egypt, just before the entry to Canaan at Gaza. This location, coupled with the unique architectural elements of Stratum IX and the rich assortment of special finds, indicate that in this era Deir el-Balaḥ was an Egyptian administrative center, perhaps with links to the very capital itself at Tell el-Amarna.

INTERMEDIATE PHASE VIII

Sandwiched between the Amarna residence of Stratum IX and the monumental fortress of Stratum VII, remains of an interim phase were discerned including a structure, floors, and four pits. This phase perhaps dates to the reign of Horemheb, though diagnostic finds are lacking. It appears that after the destruction of the Stratum IX settlement, a small interim occupation occurred, but did not constitute a major occupation level.

STRATUM VII

With the advent of the 19th Dynasty, Egypt experienced a renewed interest and involvement in her Asian holdings (Faulkner 1966). Under the capable leadership of Seti I, the strategic military and trade route running along the northern Sinai coast was refurbished through the establishment of a series of fortresses and way stations with accompanying wells or reservoirs. It is against this background of strategic renewal and construction that the remains from Stratum VII at Deir el-Balaḥ stand out in clear relief.

A dramatic change in the character of the site is reflected in the area excavated — a change which presented a well-defined and cohesive picture. Partially overlying the remains of the Amarna residence, an isolated, fortified structure was built, again adjacent to the water reservoir. The selection of the building site was clearly determined by the direct and easy proximity to the water installation from Stratum IX.

The structure itself was monumental in shape and size.

Measuring 20 m x 20 m, with fourteen rooms and a tower at each of its four corners, it most resembled a fort or tower complex. The massive mud-brick walls, preserved to a height of 1 m, served as the foundations of a structure which stood at least two stories high, while the main outer walls of the complex were 2.4 m wide. The highly indicative construction technique of a layer of sand along the base of the foundation trench, a well-known feature of Egyptian building methods, points to the Egyptian construction of this fortress.

The function and nature of this isolated structure and pond became evident in light of the Egyptian activity along the coastal route during the early 19th Dynasty. The northern Sinai route, called by the Egyptians "the Ways of Horus", was vividly depicted by Seti I on a wall relief in the Amun Temple at Karnak. Here, on the northern wall of the Great Hypostyle Hall, one of the earliest equivalents of a map depicts a series of fortresses and their accompanying wells or reservoirs running from the Egyptian frontier town of Sile (Qantara) to the Canaanite border town of Gaza. Though scholars had long been aware of this "map" and had attempted to identify the modern site or location of these ancient fortresses (Gardiner 1920), little progress was made until the last decade, when our fortress and water complex at Deir el-Balaḥ was systematically excavated. It proved to be the veritable picture-image of the depictions at Karnak and provided stark evidence for the resurgence of Egyptian military activity in Sinai and Canaan in the 13th century. The plan of the building, the "Egyptianizing" feature of the layer of sand along the base of the foundation trench (Dothan, M. 1973), and the correlation with the Seti relief indicate that the fortress was built by the 13th century. A similar fortress was discovered by the Ben Gurion University Survey near the remains of the Amarna Age site at Ḥaruvit (Oren 1980). This well-constructed fortress, built during the 19th Dynasty, may also have been one of the way stations on the "Ways of Horus".

STRATA VI-IV

Seti I was succeeded by his son Ramesses II, whose lengthy reign of sixty-six years witnessed a vast array of empire building and consolidation. These activities, in conjunction with his lengthy and costly wars against the Hittites, necessitated the upkeep and constant use of the fortresses and way stations along the northern Sinai coast.

Our first encounter with this era at the ancient site of Deir el-Balaḥ came through our excavation of the cemetery, where we recovered four anthropoid pottery coffins along with their accompanying burial gifts. These four coffins of distinctively Egyptian style form a small fraction of the over forty that surfaced through illicit diggings along with their extremely rich burial gifts, and which together comprise the largest and richest group of anthropoid coffins so far known from Canaan. Of particular interest are four locally made burial stelae, one found *in situ*, made of *kurkar* with hieroglyphic inscriptions and depictions of Mut and Osiris, strikingly similar to 19th Dynasty stelae from Deir el-Medina in Egypt.[4]

A variety of exquisite burial gifts, wrought in primarily Egyptian style, was recovered from the cemetery by our team. They included a bronze wine set, an alabaster painted goblet and a cosmetic spoon in the shape of a swimming girl, and lotus and palmette shaped beads and earrings, as well as Bes amulets, wrought in gold and carnelian. All the gifts have close analogies in New Kingdom Egypt. While the cemetery likely reflects burials from various eras grouped together, the period of Ramesses II was especially well represented and was confirmed by a seal of this Pharaoh found *in situ*. Though distinct Canaanite traits were manifest in the workmanship of some of the jewelry and in some of the common pottery vessels, the predominant culture of the people buried in the cemetery was clearly Egyptian. The combined evidence of the coffins and the burial gifts points to an affluent population steeped in Egyptian religion and culture.

Strata VI-IV of the settlement were basically contemporary with the primary use of the cemetery. The one half acre section excavated by our team exhibited a marked shift in character in this period. The water reservoir, whose use had spanned both Stratum IX and Stratum VII, was filled in and subsidiary structures were built on top. Private buildings, as well as a water-installation, heavy ash layers and kilns were excavated and indicated the transformation of the area into an industrial quarter. From the evidence at hand, the three kilns discovered by the excavation team were not used for ordinary pottery vessels; on the one hand, kiln wastes were totally lacking, and on the other hand, a large number of coffin fragments, including a coffin base and the nose from a coffin lid, were found in and around the kilns. It is likely that the coffins with their lids received an initial firing in pits built into the filled-in crater, which would account for the heavy ash layers found there. Subsequently, the lids were fired once again, this time in the kilns, which would account for the finer finish of the lids in comparison to the coffin bodies. The evidence for coffin construction at the site, therefore, is clear-cut.[5]

Alongside the coffin industry, specific finds from the settlement provided concrete evidence that many of the burial gifts were locally made and that the industrial quarter served as an artisans' quarter as well, housing a thriving and varied crafts industry. Evidence for nearly every type of burial gift was recovered including a carved-stone, reclining nude figurine (a "divine concubine" intended to accompany the dead) and *ushabti* or servant figurines, both of which had exact parallels in the cemetery; chunks of ochre for coloring the coffins and figurines; heaps of modeling clay and two identical complete molds for figurines; a heap of bronze scrap; many fragments of spinning bowls for linen weaving; and a stamp carved with the image of the god Ptah, patron of artisans.

The discovery of an ancient artisans' quarter in such close proximity to the cemetery it served is unprecedented and provides an unparalleled glimpse into mortuary industry in antiquity. It is likely that the artisans' quarter lay on the outskirts of the settlement, while the settlement of the rich patrons of the cemetery still lies buried under the dunes. In the Late Bronze Age, long before the encroachment of the Byzantine dunes, the cemetery lay only 150 m from the artisans' quarter. Together they formed a self-contained mortuary unit.

Following the flourishing Egyptian settlement of Strata VI-IV during the Ramesside era, Philistine presence at the site is indicated by a number of pits containing large quantities of typical Philistine pottery dating to the 12th-11th centuries B.C. The pits also contained a quantity of Egyptian pottery types, the sole indicators of the sounding of the final chord of Egyptian presence at the site during the early Iron Age and silent witnesses to the oft-observed pattern of the incorporation of Philistines into contemporary and former Egyptian settlements. Pits containing Israelite pottery dating to the 11th-10th centuries were excavated as well.

CONCLUSION

Deir el-Balaḥ in its various phases has served as an excellent type-site for Egyptian activity on the border of Canaan during the New Kingdom. It was founded during the Amarna Age as an Egyptian administrative center on the route to Canaan whose predominately Egyptian population experienced some interaction with the local Canaanite population (Stratum IX). During the next major phase of occupation, Stratum VII, the site was transformed into a fortified station on the "Ways of Horus", as it served to facilitate Egypt's renewed activity in Canaan during the early 19th Dynasty. In the late 19th Dynasty, it was an Egyptian-type settlement whose rich material culture was reflected in its cemetery of anthropoid pottery coffins and burial gifts. From this phase (Strata VI-IV), the excavation of an artisans' quarter for the mortuary industry associated with the cemetery has provided a rare glimpse into the technical industry connected with one of the most enlightening features of the study of any people — their burial practices.

Although the anciet indentification of Deir el-Balaḥ remains a mystery, we are able to assess from the evidence at hand that it was undoubtedly the last major outpost on the way to Gaza which, from the abundance of Egyptian records (Katzenstein 1982), was one of the most important administrative centers of the province of Canaan during the 19th Dynasty.

NOTES

1 The excavations, directed by the author, were funded in part by generous grants from the Dorot Foundation and the National Geographic Society. The core staff included Baruch Brandl, chief stratigrapher; Ann Killebrew, field supervisor; Gary Lipton, surveyor and archaeologist; Bonnie Gould, chief registrar; Hannah Bernick, assistant registrar; Ehud Netzer, architectural advisor; Shlomo Dahan, administrator; and Zeev Radovan, photographer.

   Results of the excavations of the cemetery were published in: Excavations at the Cemetery of Deir el-Balaḥ (Dothan, T. 1979). The final report of the excavations of the settlement at Deir el-Balaḥ, to be published jointly by the author and members of the core staff, will appear as a future volume of the Qedem monograph series of the Hebrew University of Jerusalem. The author would like to thank the staff for their valuable assistance, Claire Pfann for her help in preparing this article, and especially Baruch Brandl for his perceptive comments concerning the Egyptian elements at Deir el-Balaḥ dealt with in this article.

2 See the geological report by N. Bakler in the forthcoming *Qedem* volume on the excavation of the settlement at Deir el-Balaḥ.

3 See the analysis of the historical sources by P. Mayerson in the forthcoming *Qedem* volume.

4 To be published by Raphael Ventura.

5 Chemical analysis of the coffin material has also established that it is of local provenience (Dothan, Perlman, and Asaro, 1973).

REFERENCES

Aldred, C., 1971. Egypt: The Amarna Period and the End of the Eighteenth Dynasty. *CAH* (3rd ed.). Cambridge: ch. 19.

Blackman, A.M., 1937. Preliminary Report on the Excavations at Sesebi, Northern Province, Anglo-Egyptian Sudan, 1936-37. *JEA* 23:145-51.

Breasted, J.H., 1948. *A History of Egypt from the Earliest Times to the Persian Conquest* (2nd ed.). London.

Dothan, M., 1973. The Foundations of Tel Mor and Ashdod. *IEJ* 23:1-17.

Dothan, T., 1972. Anthropoid Clay Coffins from a Late Bronze Age Cemetery near Deir el-Balaḥ (Preliminary Report). *IEJ* 22:65-72.

———. 1973. Anthropoid Clay Coffins from a Late Bronze Age Cemetery near Deir el-Balaḥ (Preliminary Report II). *IEJ* 23:129-46.

———. 1979. *Excavations at the Cemetery of Deir el-Balaḥ* (Qedem 10). Jerusalem.

———. 1981a. *The Philistines and their Material Culture*. New Haven.

———. 1981b. Deir el-Balaḥ, Preliminary Report of the 1979 and 1980 Campaigns. *IEJ* 31:126-31.

———. 1982. Lost Outpost of Ancient Egypt. *National Geographic Magazine* 162:739-69.

Dothan, T., Perlman, I. and Asaro, F., 1973. Provenance of the Deir el-Balaḥ Coffins. *IEJ* 23:147-51.

Faulkner, R.O., 1966. Egypt: From the Inception of the 19th Dynasty to the Death of Ramesses III. *CAH* (3rd ed.). Cambridge: Ch. 23.

Gardiner, A.H., 1920. The Ancient Military Road between Egypt and Palestine. *JEA* 6:99-116.

Gould, Bonnie, 1982. Egyptian and Egyptianizing Pottery from Late Bronze and Early Iron Age Contexts in Canaan. Kelley, A. ed. *Papers of the Pottery Workshop, Third International Congress of Egyptology, Toronto, September 1982*. Toronto: 21-24.

Katzenstein, H.J., 1982. Gaza in the Egyptian Texts of the New Kingdom. *JAOS* 102:111-13.

Oren, E., 1973. Bir el-'Abd (Northern Sinai). *IEJ* 23:112-13.

———. 1980. Egyptian Sites from the New Kingdom in Northern Sinai. *Qadmoniot* 13:26-33 (Hebrew).

———. 1982-3. Ancient Military Roads between Egypt and Canaan. *Bulletin of the Anglo-Israel Archaeology Society*: 20-24.

ANET, Pritchard, J.R., ed. 1986. *Ancient Near Eastern Texts* (2nd ed.). Princeton.

———. 1983. Haruvit, *Hadashot Arkheyologiyot* 82:78-9 (Hebrew).

Reviv, H., 1966. The Planning of an Egyptian Campaign during the Days of Amunhotep IV. *BIES* 30:45-51 (Hebrew).

Redford, D.B., 1979. A Gate Inscription from Karnak and Egyptian Involvement in Western Asia during the Early 18th Dynasty. *JAOS* 99:270-87.

Ricke, H., 1932. *Der Grundriss des Amarna-Wohnhäuser*. Leipzig (reprinted 1967).

Ricke, H., and Borchardt, L. 1980. *Die Wohnhäuser in Tell el-Amarna*. Berlin.

Schulman, A.R., 1978. Ankhesenamun, Nofretity, and the Amka Affair. *JARCE* 15:43-48.

———. 1982. The Nubian War of Akhenaton. *L'Egyptologie en 1979, Axes prioritaires de recherches, II*. Paris: 299-316.

Several, M., 1972. Reconsidering the Egyptian Empire in Palestine during the Amarna Period. *PEA* 104:123-33.

Petrie, W.M. Flinders. 1894. *Tell el-Amarna*. London.

Weinstein, J.M., 1982. The Egyptian Empire in Palestine: A Reassessment. *BASOR* 241:1-28, esp. p. 17.

7

An Egyptological Perspective on the Exodus Narrative

Donald B. Redford

ALL nations treasure the memory of a founding figure in their remote past, hallowed by the magnitude of his accomplishment. What Arthur is to Britain, Aeneas was to Rome; Egypt had its Osiris, Athens its Agyges, the Saracens their Muhammed; and the Hebrews had their Moses. In any age of enlightenment most people who ponder soberly upon "the Man and His Age", while admitting the validity of the great myth for the self-awareness of the nation he founded, would have to admit that historically the figure and the events surrounding him do not stand up to scrutiny. With respect to Moses and his signal feat, such serious thinkers would probably agree with Sir Alan Gardiner who, over 60 years ago, spoke of the "semi-legendary, fanciful character" of the account of the event (Gardiner, 1922:215). However, times change and the wheel turns. Counterblasts, like Gardiner's, against a naive conservative acceptance of the scriptures have become a commonplace; and now it is the turn of the conservative apologist to play the part of the maverick, convincing by the very novelty of his posturing. Once again we are treated to the spectacle of the orthodox appearing as the serious scholar for whom even the chronology of the MT has veracity (Bimson, 1978).

But changing fashion has little to do with scholarship. Points of view and chains of argument cannot be ruled out just because someone declares them to be passé. Evidence long known will be just as valid as facts acquired only yesterday; and without conclusive proof of its essential rightness, the current fad cannot replace earlier points of view. In the light of these remarks, the author would like to offer some views on the Exodus narrative from the vantage point of Egyptology.

What strikes an Egyptologist first, I think, upon looking at the biblical traditions on the Exodus contained in the book of that name, is the paucity of references to the Egypt of the period. There are, both in Exodus and in Judges, no heroic Pharaohs striding like colossoi across the map of the Near East, no marching armies of conquerors, no great battles with thousands of captives, no Egyptian governors or plenipotentiaries criss-crossing the countryside of Palestine, no shipments of tribute or work hands for Egyptian coffers or estates, no cities established in Pharaoh's name. Some might feel inclined to argue, by way of explanation, that the reason why there is not more "Egyptian background" in the Exodus account is because the biblical writer has no prior interest in providing such detail, but this will not do. What is lacking in particular is the incidental reference, the parenthetic allusion, unconscious of itself, which *mutatis mutandis* one does encounter in the prophetic books when Egypt is the topic of discussion. Neither Isaiah nor Jeremiah is interested in background detail, but when they do describe something Egyptian, it is at once familiar and precise.

Now, indeed, there is a little Egyptian colouring in the Exodus account, almost wholly toponymic in nature;[1] but the Egyptologist would soon sense that it is anachronistic. The material in question comprises the names of the area Israel occupied in Egypt, the store-cities they built, and the route by which they left the country.[2] The one which sounds most familiar, viz., Ra'amses, immediately raises a problem. Toponyms incorporating the personal name *R'-ms-sw* are always compounded with some such prefixial elements as *pr-*, "house of", or *ḥwt*, "temple of": *Pr-R'-ms-sw '3-nḥtw*, "the House of Ramses Great-of-Victories", with which the Biblical city is usually identified, viz., the famous Delta residence of the Ramessides (Gauthier, 1925:102ff; Bietak, 1975: II, 179ff, 217, n. 933) almost always bears the element *pr-* in first position. In those very rare occasions when it does not, the reason is that *pr-* has been replaced by *p³ dmi n*, "The town of..." (Gardiner, 1920:137f, 137f; ef. Redford, 1963:409, n. 5). If the Exodus account had intended the famous Ramesside foundation, I am at a loss to explain why the form did not emerge as פי־רעמסס. Nor can one argue that the tradition must be authentic because the royal name in toponyms is found only in the New Kingdom, after which it passed into oblivion (Albright, 1957:255; Alt 1959:184, n. 4). *R'ms-sw* in compounds with topographic and cultic reference occurs not infrequently in the First Millennium.[3] In particular, Bubastis and its environs came to be associated with Ramesses and his House, thanks partly to the practice of post-Ramesside kings of pillaging the true site of Pi-Ramesses (Qata'na-Qantir) for blocks with which to embellish other Delta towns.

A second name intimately associated with Israel's Sojourn in Egypt is *Goshen* (Gen. 45:10, 46:28 etc.). All attempts to read into this name an Egyptian original having failed, it seems most reasonable to look for a Semitic derivation. Ever since the discovery of the prominence, nay dominance, of the Qedarite regime in the eastern Delta during the first Persian occupation of Egypt, the LXX rendering Γέσεκ Αροβιας has taken on new meaning (Albright, 1955:31). From the second Assyrian attack on Egypt under Esarhaddon (671 B.C.), the Qedarite Arabs had been able to extend their presence and their influence across the Sinai. Subsequent to the Persian conquest of Egypt, if not earlier in the 6th Century, they were able to expand northward into the

Transjordan and the Negeb and westward into the eastern Delta.[4]
It is precisely at the two extremities of this region viz., in southern
Judaea and the eastern Delta, that we encounter "the Land of
Goshen," used as a geographical designation; and it seems most
likely that this is the local, dialectical form of an original גשם, a
dynastic name in the Qedarite royal family.[5] Several toponyms
in the eastern Delta, current from the 7th Century onwards,
incorporating references to "the *H³rw*-person," or "the foreigners," would have lent themselves readily to aetiological interpretation as evidence of the sometime presence of an Asiatic
element in "Goshen".[6]

Of Succoth (Exod. 12:37, 13:20, Num. 33:5,6) and Pithom
(Exod. 1:11) a little more can be said (Redford, 1963:404f; *idem*,
1983 IV:1054f).[7] The former in all probability is a Hebraization
of Egyptian *Tjkw*, a designation of the Wady Tumilat occurring
first in the New Kingdom. In the 19th Dynasty the region was
dominated by the large fortress at Tell er-Reṭâbeh, which is
probably alluded to in Anast. vi.4.15 as the "Fortress of
Merenptah-Content-with-Truth, which is (in) *Tjkw*." By the 7th
century B.C. this settlement was in decline, if not abandoned,
and with the digging of the Red Sea canal by Necho, a new town
13 km to the east grew as an emporium and frontier post. This
was called *Pr-Itm* "of *Tjkw*," and passed into Greek as
Πιθωπ, and into Hebrew as פתם. Today it is represented by the
extensive mound of Tell el-Maskhuta. Excavations there have
confirmed that, apart from brief occupation during the Middle
Bronze, the site does not antedate the 26th Dynasty. Thereafter a
large city came into being, and numerous inscriptions confirm its
identity as Pithom.

Of course the name *pr-Itm*, "house of (the god) Atum," is of a
pattern frequently encountered from the New Kingdom on, as
attested to by several installations of that name. Only one,
however, in a New Kingdom context could with any degree of
likelihood be located in the region the Hebrews can be said to

have occupied, and identified with the store-city they are supposed to have built. This is the *pr-Itm* mentioned in Anast. vi.4.16: "we have completed the entry of the tribes of the Edomite Shasu (through) the fortress of Merneptah-Content-with-Truth, which is (in) *Tjkw*, to the pools of *pr-Itm* which (are) in *Tjkw* for the sustenance of their flocks." (Anast. iv 4.14-5.1; Gardiner 1933:76; Caminos 1954:293) Sadly, this text has been facilely used to establish the identity of this *pr-Itm* with some frontier fort in the Wadi Tumilat, which could be identified with Biblical Pithom, without noting two important points. First, it is the "*pools* of the House of Atum" (*Brkw: Wb* I 466:11; Gardiner, 1947: I:8, no. 33; Helck, 1972:511, no. 62; Osing, 1978:189) which are here located in *Tjkw*, and not necessarily the "House of Atum" itself; and second, the particular "Atum" in question is qualified as being "of Merneptah-Content-with-Truth." Now phrases involving terms for geographical features or products occupying first position in bound constructions, in which second place shows a temple name, and third a location, are quite common in ancient Egyptian texts. We see them most frequently in documents of taxation or accountancy. Thus we hear of the "grain of the estate *(rmnyt)* of the House of Amonrasonther... which is in the fields of Nefrusy," (P. Amiens vs. 5 x + 15; Gardiner, 1948:12 and *passim*) "wine of the House of Re-Harakhty of the Western River,"[8] "the great basin *(b'h)* of the Mansion of Usermare Setepenre in the House of Amun, which is on the Water of Pre," (Gauthier, 1925 II:16f.), "the vineyard of the House of Sety... in the House of Amun, which is in the district of Atum." (ibid V:187). This type of expression, indicates ownership, and the location of *the property in question,* not the proprietory institution. In each case it is the "estate," "basin," "vineyard" etc., that is being located in the area specified. The Anastasi passage no more proves the existence of a *pr-Itm* at Tell er-Reṭâbeh than Amiens papyrus proves the presence of a House of Amonrasonther at Nefrusy, or the temples of Re-Harakhty,

Ramesses II or Seṭy I in the Delta localities named. The House of
Amonrasonther, and the Temples of the two kings in question
were located at Thebes, and the Temple of Re-Harakhty at
Amarna, but such locations are not at pains to stress so obvious
a fact.

If the pattern of phrase used in Anastasi VI strongly suggests
that the *pr-Itm* lay elsewhere than in the environs of the "pools,"
the addition of Merneptah's name virtually clinches the matter.
"Atum of Merneptah-Content-with-truth" is a construction well
known to students of the cults of Ramesside times (Montet,
1932:406f; Couroyer, 1946:87f; Wildung, 1969:12f.). "The god X
of King N" is simply the allogram of the location which, in
cultic-iconographic contexts, would appear as "God X who
resides in the temple of King N." In the Ramesside period the
vast majority of such epithets (which involve primarily the royal
name "Ramesses," but occasionally also Seti, Merneptah and
even Menes) point to "guest"-cults of gods resident in royal
temples, mainly at the Delta residence, but also at Memphis or
Thebes. The Atum of Anastasi VI is in origin the Atum "who
resides in" a temple of Merneptah, probably at Pi-Ramesses.

Of the other toponyms marking Israel's route out of Egypt less
is known, but the evidence does not conflict with what has
already been said. The enigmatic "Etham" (Exod. 13:20, Num.
33:6, 7) gives the appearance of being derived from a *Ḥwt-Itm*;
and such a place does in fact occur in the Edfu nome list in
connection with the 8th nome of Lower Egypt, in the Wadi
Tumilat.[9] The LXX variant, however, in Num. 33:6 and 7, viz.
βουθαν, seems to indicate a simple distortion of "Pithom". פי־
החירות (Exod. 14:1, Num. 33:7,8) is a curious compound.
Whether a *Ḥwt-ḥrt* lies at the root of this obviously garbled form
is a moot point;[10] but if we discount the / ה as a false infix due to
the translation language, we have a name remarkably close to
P-ḫȝ-r-ti of the El-'Arish naos.[11] The name is obviously
closely related to *Ḥnt tȝ Ḥȝ-r-ti* of Demotic, which is plausibly

located in the vicinity of Lake Timsah.[12] Migdol and Baal Zephon are brought into the narrative (Exod. 14:2, Num. 33:7) to locate the encampment of the Israelites at the moment when the pursuing Egyptians caught up with them. *Migdol* is a common element in the toponomy of the eastern Delta in New Kingdom times, and enters into first position in bound constructions in which second position is occupied by a royal name (Gauthier, 1925 III:21f). Primarily the term was applied to the fortified stopping-places which lay along the route between the Egyptian frontier and Gaza, and which constituted small, rectangular keeps adjacent to water holes (Cledat, 1919:208f, Dothan, T., 1981:126f.). Migdol in the Exodus account, however, is not an element in a compound place-name, but stands alone; and there is no reason to distinguish it from the *city* of that name which, from the time of Esarhaddon, guarded the approaches to Egypt north of the Bitter Lakes.[13] From the time of the Exile part of its population was made up of Judaeans (Jer. 44:1; Padua Papiri 1, vs. 1; Fitzmyer, 1962:19) and the city undoubtedly played a role in Necho's defeat of the Babylonians in 600 (Wiseman, 1956:29f.; Lipinski, 1972:235f.). Its association in the Exodus narrative with Baal Zephon is strikingly confirmed by the Demotic geographical papyrus in which the two names occur side by side.[14]

Baal Zephon itself recalls one of the forms of Ba'al known from the Late Bronze Age, and worshipped in the Delta in Ramesside times, but also, and especially in the Late Period, when he is transmuted into Zeus Casios (cf. Sallier IV. vs. 1:3-6; Helck, 1966:2f, Stadelmann, 1967:36f; Cazelles, 1955:336f.). The Biblical allusion, however, is clearly to a cult-site which went under the name of the deity. This has long since been identified, and persuasively, with *Ras Kasrun* on the *Sebḥat Bardawil* between Lake Sirbonis and the Mediterranean. A proposed identification with Tell Defenneh (Daphnae) is wholly unwarranted, and founders on the simple fact that one would have to assume two names for the same site, Tahpanhes being the only attested scriptural designation of Daphnae.[15] Excavation at both Ras Karsun and Tell Defenneh have demonstrated neither site to be older than the Saite period.[16]

To sum up: whoever was responsible for the topographic material which now informs the stories of the Sojourn and the Exodus, be it P or even J, the configuration of the eastern Delta known to them was essentially that of the 26th Dynasty and the early Persian period. They knew of the Qedarite "Goshen," a "Land of Ramesses," and the place-names ostensibly commemorative of an erstwhile Asiatic presence in the area. The route they are familiar with is that which traverses the same tract as Necho's canal, from Bubastis to the Bitter Lakes. Then the writer moves northward in his mind's eye, past the famous town of Migdol, where men of his own race reside, to Lake Sirbonis, where Horus, in the mythical past, had already trounced Seth and thrown him out of Egypt.[17] The route is a most unlikely one, and is marked throughout by places which did not exist 480 years before Solomon's time, as the Priestly writer would date the Exodus.

But an Egyptologist would shortly make a second observation. He could not help but be impressed by the fact that, in spite of what has been said, the tradition of Israel's coming out of Egypt was an ancient and resilient one. He would soon discover that it was far older than the weak and late attempts to underpin it, by linking it with palpably anachronistic geography, had led him at first to believe. He might be encouraged, therefore, not to give up his search for evidence, and would perhaps turn next to the vast body of evidence within his own discipline, in an effort to discern even the faintest glimmer of corroboration of the Biblical account.

That in the New Kingdom large numbers of Asiatics were to be found in Egypt has, of course, long been recognised. Most of these, at least during the 18th Dynasty, arrived in the country as the result of wars of foreign conquest (Helck, 1971:107f; Fohrer, 1964:17). The P.O.W.s, sent either in shiploads or in droves by land (Gardiner, 1933:108: 15-109-1; *Urk IV* 1906: 1020:7-1021:10; P. Bologna 1086) were mainly assigned as cultivators on the great land-owning estates of the temples. With them came the "children of the chiefs," despatched to the residence for training and to be surety against their fathers' good behaviour (Alt, 1954:55; Ahituv, 1978:93f.; Vandier, 1952 IV:58f; *EA*, 156:10, 187:22f, 194:30f; *Urk* IV 949 etc.). Each was registered in a special government department (P. Lansing, 9:5; P. Bologna 1086; Wolf, 1929:94) and branded with the name of the king or god they were to serve (Kitchen, 1968 II:280:13-16; Gardiner, 1933:9:1). By the middle of the 18th Dynasty it became a cliché to speak of the great temples as "filled with male and female slaves, children of the chiefs of all the foreign lands in the captivity of his majesty... surrounded by the settlements of *Ḥ³rw*" (*Urk* IV: 1649). Their tasks are spelled out: "...to fill the (god's) ergastulum, to be weavers, to make from his byssus, fine white linen, *shrw*-linen and thick cloth; to trap and work the fields, to produce corn to fill the granary of the god's-income" (*Urk* IV: 742-13 — 473:8). Besides farming and the garment industry, the better educated captives might hope for more specialized work. Early in the empire-period we find one Asiatic was made a guardsman (*Urk* IV:1069), another a construction engineer (*Urk* IV:1468f.) yet another taken into the palace and married to the daughter of the king's barber (*Urk* IV:1369). One lucky fellow under Thutmose III became the chief design-draftsman of the Temple of Amun, and six generations later his descendants still held the post (Louvre C50; Lowle, 1976:91f.). Large numbers of foreign laborers at the disposal of the state also meant that heavy construction work could now dispense with native conscripts. Under Thutmose III fully three-fourths of the unskilled labor force at Deir el-Bahri were *Ḥ³rw*; and tomb excavation during the same reign disposed of gangs wholly composed of *Ḥ³rw* (Hayes,

1960:pl. XII:17; P. Berlin, 10621 recto, 9). Sporadically during the mid-18th Dynasty but on a much larger scale from the reign of Akhenaten, we find Asiatics (as well as Nubians) in the Egyptian armed forces as spearmen, shield-bearers, swordsmen, charioteers, etc. (Davies, 1908 I:pl. 15; II:pl. 31; Habachi, 1954:508f.) and from the same period Levantine elements begin to invade government offices, the priesthood (Berlin, 1284), the merchant class (P. Bologna, 1094:10-3; Gardiner, 1933:9-10) and later even service in the palace (Helck, 1971:353f.).

In the wake of the new Asiatic labor force came varying numbers of their compatriots, voluntarily seeking what Egypt had to offer. This is nothing new, though the evidence is now more explicit. A merchant class appears in the late 18th and early 19th Dynasties, and communities of Canaanites begin to take shape around shrines to their native gods (Helck, 1966:2f; Stadelman, 1967:36f.). Canaanite names, and those inspired by the presence of Canaanites, increase in the *onomasticon*, and Canaanite dialects are heard within the land (Helck, 1971:505f.). Indeed, "to do business speaking the *Ḫ³rw*-tongue" comes to be a synonym for "to haggle" (Janssen, 1961:59:14,13). In the Delta the usual groups of Canaanite pastoralists are allowed to enter with their livestock, as they had for centuries past (Gardiner, 1933:76f; *idem*, 1953:7, fig. 2). But they kept pretty much to themselves, and fraternization with these tribesmen was considered beneath the sophisticated, city-bred, Egyptian (Černy, 1955:161f.; Anast. I:20,2-4).

This range of evidence does not give much cheer to those craving specifics. Apart from the nature of the descent into Egypt, viz., by pastoralists seeking grazing land, and a vague similarity between the Hebrews in bondage and the occupation of the levies of Canaanite P.O.W.s, there are no echoes of the historicity of the tradition. For one thing, the New Kingdom texts neither tell of, nor hint at, the existence of a subjected ethnic element, resident (according to one of the Pentateuchal sources) in one part of the country, which had become so large as to be an object of apprehension to the Egyptian state. As the writer has pointed out elsewhere (Redford, 1970:232f.), the threat of invasion from the east which, both in the Joseph story and the Exodus account, makes credible Joseph's accusation of spying and Pharaoh's fear that the Israelites would collaborate with an invader, makes no sense at all in a New Kingdom context. At that time Palestine and most of Syria constituted an Egyptian dependency; and during the Hebrew monarchy Egypt's northern border was buffered by the friendly Hebrew and Philistine states. For the Late Period, however, and especially from 671 B.C. on, it is a most plausible motivation for the plot of the story. Faced in succession across the Sinai with a hostile Assyria, Babylonia and Persia, the Egypt of the 26th Dynasty was greatly exercised about the security of her eastern marches in precisely those regions the Israelites were supposed to have inhabited.

A second cause of puzzlement has to do with the tasks the Egyptians are supposed to have set their Hebrew servants to fulfil. These do not sound authentic. Brickyards functioned and flourished during the New Kingdom, and we have some of the administrative texts from such work places (Černy, 1963:38f.), but there is no evidence that Asiatics were traditionally employed in *this* kind of labor (whereas they are ubiquitous in *heavy* construction work).[19] As for the ערי־מסכנות the Hebrews are supposed to have built, elsewhere in the Bible they are a purely Hebrew institution (cf. I Kings 9:19, II Chron. 8:4-6, 16:4, 17:12), unknown to Pharaonic Egypt.[20]

In the third place, the progressive assimilation, as the New Kingdom draws to a close, of Asiatic elements into the society of the country is not reflected in the Biblical narrative, where the Hebrews live apart and, when ejected, can leave *en bloc*. One cannot deny the *possibility* that behind an historical allusion in New Kingdom texts to a group of H^3rw, *'apiru* or $\check{S}^3sw$, there lurk the ancestral Hebrews; but in sum it seems to me only plausible when the allusion is to a group already located in Canaan.

If the New Kingdom texts have proven, upon inspection, to be barren of corroborative evidence, is there no reference at all, during *any* part of the Pharaonic period, to the Sojourn and Exodus? In fact, of course, there is; but it is late enough to attract unto itself the accusation of being merely the contemporary, Egyptian reaction to the Hebrew accounts themselves. I refer to the compositions, circulating under various names, which spring to our attention from the late 4th Century B.C. on (Redford, 1983:ch. 8; Text in: Stern, 1974, I).

Two great themes involving foreigners had already inspired certain narratives in the New Kingdom, viz., the Hyksos expulsion and the Egyptian empire. But the problems which might have attended the presence in Egypt of a large community of foreigners never surfaced in the literature of the period; and xenophobia as a core around which narratives might have taken root is not prominent.

Six hundred years later, however, the picture changes. With the repeated and successful invasion of Egypt from the 7th Century on, and the growing presence of alien communities brought in as merchants or mercenaries, several pieces of folklore emerged which betray an underlying self-conscious apprehension about the northerner and what he is able to do to Egypt. A plague is said to have ravaged the land. The cause is isolated as the presence of undesirable aliens and/or "leprous" people. These were forthwith expelled, usually towards the north, where they turn up as the ancestors of contemporary peoples. By the late 4th Century this "Plague/Expulsion" motif had achieved a wide currency in oral and literary tradition, in derision of the many foreigners Egypt now had to deal with. A second topos which appears in narrative, thanks to the Kushite-Assyrian *contretemps* and the trauma of the Persian invasions, is the motif of "Invasion from the North/Deliverance from the South." A group of northerners, predicted in most accounts by an unusual prophetic oracle, invades Egypt and drives Pharaoh, his family and court to flight. The invaders quickly occupy the land, and destroy cities and temples. With the help of the gods and a newly-conscripted army, Pharaoh appears out of Nubia (whither he had fled), drives the enemy back to Asia and purifies Egypt. In the jingoistic atmosphere created by the Persian stand-off of the 4th Century and the forlorn nationalism of Ptolemaic times, this plot-pattern was used time and again in a mythological or early historical setting.

The two themes are united in a story which Manetho incorporates in the text of his *Aegyptiaca* II.[21] The story centered upon one Osarsiph, consciously interpreted as Moses, and became increasingly influential in the Judaic-pagan polemic which dominated intellectual debate in the Ptolemaic period. In fact, however, the Manethonian romance is connected with the Hebrew Exodus only secondarily. All the evidence indicates that the putative Demotic original Manetho used, though perhaps written not many generations before his time, ultimately derived from an old aetiology of *Amarna period monuments* in Upper Egypt, and had nothing to do with Moses and the Israelites. The connection came about through the need felt by the Egyptians to rationalize the Hebrew traditions which in the 4th Century they were becoming aware of, by calling upon traditional motifs of their own.

Our conclusions to this point may be summarized as follows: *1.* The account of the Bondage and Exodus, as it now stands in the Book of Exodus, contains little if any material, historical, literary or folkloristic, which may be said to be of Egyptian origin.

2. The little topographical information the narrative contains points without exception to the Saite or Persian period as the time of origin.

3. The few specifics which describe the nature of the Bondage in Exodus do not square with what is known of the origin, composition, status and function of the Asiatic element in Egypt during the New Kingdom.

4. Egyptian tales of an Asiatic descent into Egypt followed by an expulsion have no independent value as a witness to the Hebrew tradition.[22]

The further conclusion is, I think, virtually forced upon us that the present version of the account in Exodus is a post-Exilic composition which, in the absence of genuine historical detail, was obliged to draw on contemporary toponymy: but to draw such a conclusion is not, needless to say, tantamount to branding the Biblical tradition a wholly late fabrication. When all is said, the following points remain unassailable:

1. There was an early and strong reminiscence of a voluntary descent into Egypt by pastoralists, in which one Jacob played a leading part, and was later to achieve a reputation as an ancestral figure.

2. Those who made the descent had not only prospered and multiplied, but had also for a time become exceedingly influential in Egypt.

3. Subsequently, strong antipathy had arisen between the autochthonous inhabitants and the Asiatic newcomers.

4. This had resulted in the enforced retirement of the intrusive element to the Levantine littoral whence they had emerged.[23]

The only chain of *historical* events which will fit this vague reminiscence in late tradition is the Hyksos descent into and occupation of Egypt. The memory of this epochal movement must have lived on among the Semitic-speaking inhabitants of the area whence the chieftains who had descended to the Nile had emerged, and whither their progeny, four or five generations later, had retired. This area, as is now known, is the southern coast lands of the eastern Mediterranean, called in Egyptian *Dj³hy* and *Ḥ³rw*, i.e., Palestine and the Phoenician coast. Here the tradition took shape of the great ancestral figure Jacob (possibly derived ultimately from the Hyksos potentate)[24] the divine promise of a sojourn in Egypt, the 4-generation span, the recollection of having been a great nation, etc. Here emerged also the rationalized account of the retreat from Egypt: it had not been a military defeat in battle and an ignominious expulsion, but the salvation of innocents from tyranny, told with folkloristic panache at the expense of the Egyptians. It is, as it were, the "Hyksos" version of events that we are listening to (Gardiner, 1922:204). In fact, in the Exodus account we are confronted by the tradition of those events to which the *entire* Semitic-speaking population of Palestine and Syria had fallen heir, and which, as subsequent events were to transpire, was preserved in the lore of only one, small and peripheral part of that population,viz., the Shasu, the ancestral Hebrews. Originally at home on the south-eastern fringe of the Levant, these predatory tribesmen had long been one of the principal elements of resistance to Pharaonic encroachment, and owed no allegiance to Egypt. Their eventual westward movement and peaceful settlement among the Canaanite cities[25] resulted in the adoption by the new-comers of the more sophisticated traditions long since the intellectual baggage of the urban civilization they and others were in the process of supplanting during the 13th and 12th Centuries.

NOTES

1   By and large the thematic material at the outset of the book of Exodus, viz., the birth narrative and the bondage, owes little to a specific Egyptian source (cf. D.B. Redford, 1967:20911 and Irvin, 1977:19ff.). The plagues are in keeping with phenomena which *can* be witnessed in the Nile Valley (Hart, 1957:84ff.; 1958:48ff.), but many motifs appear elsewhere as well (cf. Kramer, 1949:399ff. and Dumermuth, 1964:323ff.). Attempts to read Egyptian symbolism into the crossing of the sea and to find a real connection between ים-סוף and the *sht-i³rw* (cf. Towers, 1959:150ff.) are more ingenious than convincing. It has long been recognized that the crossing motif owes a good deal to the Jordan crossing (cf. Coats, 1967:261; 1969:17; Childs, 1970:414f). In fact, there may be a hint in the role of the Sea of the rapacious character of Yam (Gray, 1965:22ff.; Cross

and Freedman, D.N., 1955:239; Childs *op. cit.*:413). On the "Sea" in Egyptian literature, see Helck (1980:1276ff).

2   Discussions on the toponymy of the Sojourn and Exodus often become enmeshed in, or founder on, the prior considerations of a long versus a short route, the number of "exodoi," the role of the P-redactor in contradistinction to the early traditions, etc., (for the routes as outlined by J, E and P see Noth 1962:105ff.; Fohrer (1964:98ff. and Childs, 1970:407ff) for a refreshing *caveat*, see Simons (1959:235). The present investigation will refrain from making a prior division into sources a canon of evaluation.

3   *Pr-R'mssw*: Gardiner (1947:171*f no. 410), Montet (1938:141), Borchardt (1930: nos. 689, 700); ḥwt-ntr nsw R'-mc-sw: Buhl (1959: E, b, 9; F, a, 16); Gardiner (1918:130), God X n R'-ms-sw: Naville (1891: pl. 36, 46); Tresson (1934:820, line 28; cf. line 13: *thr n Wsr-m³-'t-r'*); for "Ramesses" in the Theban cult during the 21st Dynasty, see Legrain (1908:77; 1914: 42224, n, 5-6). The title "King's-son of Ramesses" is of a cultic pattern (Schmitz, 1976:276ff) and has nothing to do with the toponym *Pr-r'-ms-sw*: (Couroyer, 1946:87ff; 1954:108ff; Alt: 180, n. 3). For the prominence of the Ramessides at Bubastis, see Habachi (1957:112ff. and *passim*). With respect to the tradition of a "land" of Ramesses (Gen. 47:11), cf. the appellation of the agricultural district of the Bubastite nome, viz., the "Divine Tract" *(sht-ntr)*: Goyon (1972:100, nn. 174-5). Of more importance may be the name of the old 23rd Dynasty bailiwick, from Bubastis to Tanis and Sile, between the Tanitic and Pelusiac branches. From the 8th Century B.C. to Roman times this was considered a territorial unit, and received the designation *R'-nfr* (pronounced probably *Ra'-nuf*): Piankhy Stela 19, 114 (Gauthier, 1925: I:190; III:130; Kamal, 1905:187; Daressy, 1914:35f. (the district of *R'-nfr* linked with *sht-Dint*, the שדה־צען of Psalm 78:12, 43); Montet, 1946:64, pl. 15 *Edfu* I:130f; p. Dem. Cairo 31169, rct. ii 4; Vandier, 1965:169ff.; Helck, 1974:190). One wonders whether it has influenced the belief in the existence of an erstwhile "Land of Ramesses" in the area.

4   (Wiseman, 1956:31f; Dumbrell, 1971:38ff; J.M. Myers, 1971:379; Van Seters, 1975:266).

5   Baumgartner, 1967 I:197f. For the frequency of the name in Lihyanite (Winnett, Reed, 1970:114ff.) several kings bear this name (*ibid.*, 116, n. 25), and there is no reason to restrict ourselves to the Gashmu whose son made the Tell el-Maskhuta dedications (Rabinowitz, 1956:1ff). On the genealogy (Lemaire, 1974:63ff., 70, n. 41).

6   Redford, 1973:17; cf. especially *ḫ³śt* (Gauthier, 1925 IV:15); *Ḥ³styw* (locations doubtful: Caminos, 1972:222); *t³- ḥwt ḫ³swt* (near Bilbeis: P. Dem. Cairo 31169, ii.25); *p³- sbty n p³- ḫ³rw* near Athribis (Gauthier, 1925 V:25).

7 Gauthier and Sottas saw in *Tjkw* an African word *thukka*, meaning "pasturage": (Gauthier, 1925:14, n. 1); Albright, however, declares it North-west Semitic: (Albright, 1969:155).

8 Petrie, 1894: pl. 25:91; Peet and others, 1922 I: pl. 64:46-8, 1933 II: pl. 38:8; 1951 III: pl. 86-44, 87:68 and *passim*; Hayes, 1951:14, fig. 4:10; 46, fig. 6:54 and *passim*.

9 *Edfu* VI, 39. Any connection between אתם and Egyptian *ḥtm*, "fortress" (Cazelles, 1955:357ff), is a pure flight of fancy. The laryngeal in initial position in this word was strong (cf. *WWTM*: Černy, 1976:255f.); and Hebrew did not elide *ḥ* in such cases. Cf. חתם Egyptian *ḥtm*, "to seal"; חתמת *ḥtmt*, "signet ring"; חריט *ḥrt*, "sack". Theoretically possible would be an equation with *Itmt* in the region of Lake Borollos, where Osiris, Harendotes and their coterie of gods were worshipped (Daressy, 1917:276ff; Serrin, 1948:332), although this appears to be too remote a site to be considered.

10 Cazelles, 1955:350f., *ḥwt-ḥrt*, Caminos, 1959: pl. 6,3:14. The sequence of place names is of some interest: [   ] *d'w*, *Hwt-w'rt*, *Ḥwt-ḥrt*, *Ḥwt-ḥrt*, *W³-wt-Ḥr*. The sequence is clearly down the Pelusiac branch, ending at the north-east frontier. "Upper and Lower Mansions" sounds a trifle artificial, but they may be playful (?) derivations from *Pr-Ḥwt-ḥr*, a place in the environs of Pi-Ramesses mentioned in Anast. iii.3.3 and the Nitocris Adoption stela, 254 (Gardiner, 1920:186; Caminos, 1957:80; Caminos, 1964:93).

11 Wady el-'Arish Naos, C, 6: Goyon, 1934, 14, Tefnut, bereaved of her husband Shu, goes to the palace of Shu at noon, "...and then the Majesty of [Geb (her son) saw her (?)], and he found her in this place the name of which is *P³--h³-rty*. Thereupon he seized her and raped her." Here the toponym is interpreted as the "Place of the Widow", with reference to the widowed goddess.

12 P. Dem. Cairo 31169.iii.18 (Cazelles, 1955:351) for the literature. I am doubtful whether Pi-hahirot *(P³--h³-rty)* is to be equated with *Ḥ³rm*, the *mw* of L.E. 8 (Anast. v.II.4; *Edfu* I, 322:Iv, 27; *Dendera* I, 125; de Wit, 1938:192; Posener, 1937: pl. V. 77 n.e.), probably the watery tracts west of Tell er-Reṭâbeh. The *Ḥ³rm* was undoubtedly incorporated somehow into the canal system of Necho (the *ḥnt nt i³btt* of Pithom Stela, 10, [16], 19 etc.); and *P-h³rty*, if *Pi-* corresponds to *r³*, "mouth", may also ultimately derive from a term applied to a waterway. Note Albright's assumption of a semitic folk-etymology for Pi-hahiroth "mouth of the canals," (Albright, 1948:16).

13 So already (Gardiner, 1922:212; Mallon, 1921:167f., 194). Most probably the site is to be identified with Tell el-Ḥer, 15 km south of Pelusium (cf. *ANET²*, 292). Cledat's sondage there revealed occupation from Saitic to Roman times: (Cledat, 1920:193f.). There is simply no justification for

rejecting the identification out of hand (Cazelles, 1955:344ff.; Simons, 1959:348, n. 214). Attempts to find the Migdol of the Prophets and the Saite texts already in existence in Amarna times, involve a misunderstanding of *EA* 234:28-30: *amurme* URU *Ak-ke*ki *kima* URU *Ma-aq-da-li*ki¹ *ina* KUR *Misri*. This should be rendered, "see! Accho is like a tower in Egypt!" (i.e., firm and secure), treating the form as the common noun מגדל, the lent of URU *dannati / dannuti* in Akkadian [*Chicago Assyrian Dictionary* III:89ff].

14   P. Dem. Cairo 31169. iii.22. In the same context occur "Migdol" (iii.20), "Migdol of the region of thorn bushes(?)" (iii.21), and "Migdol Pohay" (iii.23) (Daressy, 1911:7).

15   For Ras Kasrun (Abel, 1949:232f; Cazelles, 1955:332ff) for full bibliography and discussion. Cf. in particular Eissfeldt, 1932; Noth, 1962:109f. Casios probably is derived from *hṯyn* (חסן "stronghold") of Anast. i.27. 4. For the identification with Daphnae (Albright, 1950:1ff). Note that Daphnae is given an entry separate from Baal Sephon in the Demotic Geographical Papyrus: 31169, ii.18.

16   For Ras Kasrun I am indebted to the oral communication of Professor E. Oren (Dothan, 1968:255f; *idem*, 1969:48f). For Tell Defenneh, Petrie, 1888: pl. 22 earliest deposit Psammetichus I) *Loc. cit.*: p. 61) earliest pottery, prototypical of Naukratis forms, *Loc. cit.*: p. 65) native wares of 26th Dynasty date). Most reasonably understood, the evidence dictates that we construe Daphnae as a Saite foundation staffed with foreign troops to guard the eastern approaches to the Delta (Boardman, 1964:150f). A chance remark of Petrie's (Petrie, 1888:47) that some "red (fired?) bricks" resembled "Ramesside" bricks was seized upon confidently (Aime-giron, 1940:445) as evidence that the site was in existence in the New Kingdom! In the complete absence of corroborative ceramic or epigraphic evidence, such a conclusion is nonsense. From the writer's own excavations in Egypt many fired bricks have come to light resembling "Ramesside" bricks; but they are 21st Dynasty (10th Century) in date, and are *all* found re-used in Saite contexts!

17   Herodotus iii.5. 3. On the generally inferior geographical knowledge conveyed by the Exodus account, Gardiner, 1922:215; North, 1947:181f. This paper is not concerned with the exact site of the crossing of the "sea", nor the identity of the latter (Davies, 1979:ch. 7). From the route already established, it must be a more northerly body of water, rather than the gulf of Suez; but whether the common equation of ים סוף with Egyptian *tjwfy* (Gardiner, 1922:212; *idem*, 1947 II:201; Cazelles, 1955:340ff) is correct, is a moot point: (Simons, 1959:77f., 235f). For *tjwfy*, "papyrus" in Egyptian (Černy, 1976:332; Meeks, 1980:425).

18   Cf. the illustrious Yanhamu of the Amarna Letters.

19   The 'Apiru in particular engage in construction work, but they are also

found in agricultural pursuits. (Van Seters, 1975:26ff, and n. 51; Miller, 1977:248ff; Thompson, 1974:184ff). There is a general consensus today that the ancestral Hebrews are not to be sought in the 'Apiru: (Rainey, 1980:251).

20 As Professor Van Seters has pointed out to me (oral communication) the use of the מס imposed on a foreign element in a population reflects Hebrew practice under the monarchy; on the *corvée* in Israel (Mendelsohn, 1962:31ff; Avigad, 1980:170ff).

21 The account was probably not authored by Manetho himself (although he might have edited or adapted it), but was found among the temple-library records he so liberally used. It is becoming increasingly clear that, although Manetho was in possession of the ongoing King-list tradition of which the Turin Canon is an exemplar one millemmium older, the priestly historian interspersed his list with numerous historical romances translated from Demotic originals.

22 It seems to me, therefore, that any modern historical interpretation which depends heavily on the details of this Exodus tradition is at once both naive and gratuitous, if not downright dishonest. Debate over one or two Exodoi (de Vaux, 1973:349f; Schmid, 1965:260f; Malamat, 1973:88f) or which tribes may or may not have taken part (Eissfeldt, 1975 II: ch. 26) is wholly fanciful and cannot be taken seriously.

23 Whether or not the "Deliverance at the Sea" is the kernel of the Exodus tradition (Noth, 1962:104f; Fohrer, 1964:97f); the formula regarding bringing Israel up from Egypt seems to be early and possibly tied in with the Israelite cult: (Coats, 1967:259, n. 6; *idem*, 1969:10; Noth, 1971:47f); but cf. Thompson, 1974:174f; Van Seters, 1975:143 and the literature there cited. For the Red Sea tradition in early Israel (Norin, 1977:105f). That the Song of the Sea is of early date has long been argued by Freedman: 1955:239, *idem*, 1975:3f.

24 On the very common appearance of Ya'gob + DN in Hyksos inscriptions, see the full discussion and bibliography in Thompson, 1974:47ff; Ward, 1976:358f, 61cf.

25 That it is to the Shasu that scholars should look if they wish to investigate the origins of the Hebrews, has become increasingly clear since Helck's study on the bedu incursions of the 19th Dynasty (Helck, 1968:472ff) and Giveon's epochal work on the Shasu (Giveon, 1971). Their gradual movement into the Negeb and central Palestine from their original home in Transjordan in the 13th and 12th Centuries is the historical reality behind the "Conquest" tradition, and is increasingly being reflected in the evidence regarding the *peaceful* nature of the occupation: (Fritz, 1981: 61ff). For further literature and discussion, see Redford 1982:74, n. 155; Rainey, 1980:251).

REFERENCES

Abel, F.M., 1940. Les Confins de la Palestine et de l'Egypte sous les Ptolemees (fin). *R.B.* 49: 224-339.

Ahituv, S., 1978. Economic Factors in the Egyptian Conquest of Canaan. *IEJ* 28: 39-108.

Aime-Giron, N., 1940. Ba'al Saphon et les dieux de Tahpanhes dans un nouveau Papyrus Phenicien. *ASAE* 40: 433-460.

Albright, W.F., 1948. The Early Alphabetic Inscriptioms from Sinai and their Decipherment. *BASOR* 109:6-22.

———. 1950. Baal Zaphon in Baumgartner. W, Eissfeldt. O, Elliger. K. Rost L. (eds.). 1950 *F.S. A Bertholet*. Tübingen.

———. 1955. New Light on Early Recensions of the Hebrew Bible. *BASOR* 140: 27-33.

———. 1957. *From the Stone Age to Christianity*. New York.

———. 1969. *Yahweh and the Gods of Canaan*. New York.

Alt, A., 1954. Neue Berichte über Feldzüge von Pharaonen des Neuen Reiches nach Palastina. *ZOPV* 70: 31-75.

———. 1959. *Kleineschriften zur Geschichte des Volkes Israel* III. München.

Avigad, N., 1980. The Chief of the Corvée. *IEJ* 30: 170-173.

Baumgartner, W., 1967. *Hebraisches und Aramaisches Lexikon zum A.T.* I Leiden.

Bietak, M., 1975. *Tell ed-Dab'a. II*, Wien.

Bimson, J.J., 1978. *Redating the Exodus and Conquest*. Sheffield.

Boardman, J., 1964. *The Greeks Overseas*. Harmondsworth.

Borcharat, L., 1930. *Statuen und Statuetten*. (CCO) Cairo.

Buhl, M.L., 1959. *The Late Egyptian Anthropoid Stone Sarcophagi*. Copenhagen.

Caminos, R.A., 1957. *Late Egyptian Miscellanies*. London.

———. 1959. *Literary Fragments in the Hieratic Script*. Oxford.

———. 1964. The Nitocris Adoption Stela. *JEA* 50: 71-101.

———. 1972. Another Hieratic Manuscript from the Library of Pwerem son of Kiki (pap. B.M. 10288). *JEA* 58: 206-224.

Cazelles, H., 1955. Les localisations de l'Exodus et la Critique Literaire. *R.B.* 62: 321-364.

Černy, J., 1955. Reference to Blood Brotherhood Among Semites in an Egyptian Text of the Ramesside Period. *JNES* 14: 161-163.

———. 1976. *Coptic Etymological Dictionary.* Oxford.

Chassinat, E., Daumas, F., 1934-1965. *Le Temple de Dendera.* 6 vols. Cairo.

Childs, B.S., 1970. The Red Sea Tradition. *V.T.* 20: 406-418.

Cledat, M.J., 1920. Notes sur l'isthme de Suez (suit) *BIFAO* 18: 167-197.

Coats, G.W., 1967. The Tradio-historical Character of the Red Sea Motif. *V.T.* 17: 253-265.

———. 1969. The Song of the Sea. *CBQ* 31: 1-17.

Couroyer, B., 1946. La residence ramesside du Delta et la Ramses bibliqe. *R.B.* 53: 75-98.

———. 1954. Dieux et fils de Ramses. *RB* 61: 108-117.

Cross, F.M., Freedman, D.N., 1955. The Song of Miriam. *JNES* 14: 237-250.

Daressy, G., 1914. Sarcophages d'El-Qantarah. *BIFAO* 11: 29-38.

———. 1917. La porte de beltim. *ASAE* 17: 276-278.

Davies, N., de G., 1908. *The Rock Tombs of El-Amarna.* London.

Davies, G.I., 1979. *The Way of the Wilderness: A Geographical Study of the Wilderness Itineraries of the Old Testament.* Cambridge.

de Vaux, R., 1973. *Histoire Ancienne d'Israel.* Paris.

de Wit, C., 1958. *Les Inscriptions du temple d'Opet.* Bruxelles.

Donadoni, S., (ed.). 1963. *Le fronti indisetti della storia egiziana.* Rome.

Dothan, M., 1968. Lake Sirbonis (Sabkhat el-Bardawil). *IEJ* 18: 255-256.

———. 1969. An Archaeological Survey of Mt. Casius and its Vicinity in *Eretz-Israel* 9: 47-60.

Dothan, T., 1981. Deir-el-Balah, 1979-80. *IEJ* 31: 126-131.

Dumermuth, F., 1964. Folkloristisches in der Erzählung von den Ägyptischen plagen. *ZAW* 76:323-325.

Dumbrell, 1971. The Tell-el-Maskhuta. *BASOR* 203: 33-44.

Eissfeldt, O., 1932. *Baal-Zaphon, Zeus Kasios und der Durchzig der Israeliten durchs Meer.* Halle.

———. 1975. Palestine in the Time of the Nineteenth Dynasty. a. The Exodus and Wandering. *CAH* Vol. II/2. ch. 26.

Fitzmyer, J.A.S., 1962. The Padua Aramaic Papyrus Letters. *JNES* 211: 15-24.

Fohrer, G., 1964. *Überlieferung und Geschichte des Exodus.* Berlin.

Freedman, D.N., 1975. Early Israelite History in the Light of Early Israelite Poetry. *In* Geodicke, H., Roberts, J.J.M.

158   *Donald B. Redford*

————. 1975. *Unity and Diversity*. Baltimore & London.

Fritz, V., 1981. The Israelite Conquest in the Light of Recent Excavations at
Khirbet-el-Meshash. *BASOR* 241: 61-74.

Gardiner, A.H., 1918. The Delta Residence of the Ramessides. *JEA* 5: 179-200.

————. 1922. The Geography of the Exodus. In *Recueil d'etudes
égyptologiques dédiées à la mémoire de J.-F. Champollion*. Paris: 203-215.

————. 1933. *Late Egyptian Miscellanies*. Brussels.

————. 1947. *Ancient Egyptian Onomastica*. 2. Oxford.

————. 1948. *Ramessie Administrative Documents*. Oxford.

————. 1953. The Memphite Tomb of the General Haremhab. *JEA* 39: 3-12.

Gauthier, H., 1925-1931. *Dictionnaire des noms geographiques contenus dans
les textes hieroglyphiques*. 7 Vols. Cano.

————. 1925. *Un decret trilingue en l'noneur de Ptolemee*. IV. Cairo.

Giveon, R., 1971. Les bedouins Shosou des documents egyptiens. Leiden.

Goedicke, H., Roberts, J.J.M., (eds.). 1975. *Unity and Diversity*. Baltimore.

Goyon, J.C., 1972. *Confirmation du pouvoir royal au nouvel empire*. Cairo.

Gray, J., 1965. *The Legacy of Canaan*. Leiden.

Habachi, L., 1954. Khanta'na-Qantir: Importance. *ASAE* 52: 443-562.

————. 1959. *Tell Basta*. Cairo.

Hayes, J.H., Thompson, J.M., 1977. *Israelite & Judean History*. Philadelphia.

Hayes, W.C., 1951. Inscriptions from the Palace of Amenhotep III. *JNES* 10:
35, 82, 156, 231.

————. 1960. A Selection of Thutmoside Ostraca from Deir-el-Bahri. *JEA* 46:
29-52.

Helck, W. 1966. Zum Auftreten Fremder Götter in Ägypten. *Oriens Atiquus* 5:
1-14.

————. 1968. Die Bedrohung Palastinas durch einwandernde gruppen an
ende der 18 und anfang der 19 Dynastie. *VT.* 18: 472-480.

————. 1971. *Die Beziehungen Agyptens zur Vorderasien im 3 und 2
Jahrtausend*. Wiesbaden.

————. 1972. *Die Beziehungen Ägyptens zur Vorderasien*. Wiesbaden.

————. 1974. *Die altägyptische Gaue*. Wiesbaden.

————. 1980. Meer. *LdA* III: 1275-1279.

Hart, G., 1957. The Plagues of Egypt I. *ZAW.* 69: 84-102.

————. 1958. The Plagues of Egypt II. *ZAW.* 70: 48-59.

Irvin, D., Thompson, T.L., 1977. The Joseph & Moses Narratives in Hayes,

J.H., Miller, J.M., (eds.). 1977. *Israelite and Judean History*. Philadelphia.

Janssen, J.M.A., 1961. *Two Ancient Egyptian Shipdogs*. Leiden.

Kamal, A., 1905. *Steles Ptolemaiques et romainen*. (C.C.G.). Cairo.

Kitchen, K.A., 1968. *Ramesside Inscriptions*. Oxford.

Kramer, S.N., 1949. Blood-Plague Motif in Sumerian Mythology. *Archiv Orientalni* 17: 399-405.

Legrain, G., 1908.

———. 1914. *Stat et Statuettes*. (C.C.G.). Cairo.

Lemaire, A., 1974. Un Mouveau arabe de Qedar dans l'inscription de l'autel a encens de Ladish. *R.B.* 81: 63-72.

Lipinski, E., 1972. The Egypto-Babylonian War of the Winter 601-600 B.C. Annali del Instituto Orientali di Napoli 22(32).

Lowle, D.A., 1976. A Remarkable Family of Draughtsmen-Painters from Early Nineteenth Dynasty Thebes. *Oriens Antiquus* S:91-106.

Malamat, A., 1973. C/R de Vaux, *Histoire Ancienne d'Israël*. *R.B.* 80: 82-92.

Mallon, A., 1921. *Les Hebreux en Egypte*. Rome.

Meeks, D., (ed.). 1980. *Anee Lexicographique* I. Paris.

Mendelsohn, I., 1962. On Corvée Labor in Ancient Canaanite Israel. *BASOR* 167:31-53

Miller, J.M., 1977. The Israelite Occupation of Canaan. Pp. 213-284 of Hayes, J.H., and Miller, J.M., Israelite and Judean History. Philadelphia: Westminster Press.

Montet, P. 1932. in.

———. 1938. Trois Gouverneurs de Tonis *kemi* 7:123-159.

———. 1946. Inscriptions de basse epoque trouvées a Tanis *Kemi* 8: 29-126.

Myers, J.M., 1971. In *Albright Festschrift*. Baltimore.

Naville, E., 1891. *Bubastis*. London.

Norin, S.I.L., 1977. *Er Spaltete das Meer: Die Auszugsüberlieferung in Psalmen und Kult des alten Israel*. Lund.

North, C.R., 1947. The Essenee of Idolatry. In Henperl, J., Rost, L. (eds.). *Von Ugarit Nach Qumran. Beitrage zur Alttestamentalichen und Altorientalischen forschung Eissfeldt O.* Halle.

Noth, M., 1962. *Exodus*. London.

———. 1972. *A History of the Pentateuchal Traditions*. Englewood Cliffs.

Oppenheim, A.L., Reiner, E., Biggs, R.D. (eds.). 1959. *The Assyrian Dictionary*. Chicago.

Osing, J., 1978. Review of Cerny, J. 1976. Coptic Etymological Dictionary. *JEA* 64: 186-189.

Peet, T.E., 1922-1951. *The City of Akhnaten*, 3 Vols. London.

Petrie, W.M.F., 1888. *Tanis part II, Nebeshe (Am) and Defenneh (Thahpanhes)*. London.

———. 1894. *Tell-el-Amarna*. London.

Posener, G., 1937. *La premiere domination Perse en Egypte*. Cairo.

Rabinowitz, I., 1956. Aramaic Inscriptions of the 5th Century B.C. from a North Arab Shrine in Egypt.*JNES* 15: 1-9.

Rainey, A.F., 1980. Review of Bimson, J.J. 1978. Redating the Exodus and Conquest. *IEJ* 30: 249-251.

Redford, D.B., 1963. Exodus I 11, *V.T.* 13: 401-418.

———. 1967. The Literary Motif of the Exposed Child. (c.f. Ex. 11:1-10). *Numen* 14: 209-228.

———. 1970. *A Study of the Biblical Joseph Story*. Leiden.

———. 1973. Studies in Relations Between Palestine and Egypt During the first Millenium B.C.: II The Twenty Second Dynasty. *JAOS* 93: 3-17.

———. 1983. *King Lists, Annals and Daybooks: A Contribution to Egyptian Historiography*. Toronto.

———. 1983. Pithom. *Ld'ef* IV: 1054-1058.

Rochemoteix, Le Marquis de. 1929-1934. Le Temple d'Edfu I. *MMAF* 21-31.

Reed, W.L., Winnett, F.V. 1970. *Ancient records from North Arabia*. Toronto.

Schmid, R., 1965. Meerwunder- und Landnahme-Traditionen. *Theologische Zeitschrift* 21: 260-268.

Schmitz, B., 1976. *Untersuchungen zum Titel S3-Nswt "köngssohn"*. Bonn.

Sethe, K., 1906-1909. *Urkunden de 18 Dynastie (Urkunden des ägyptischen Altertums IV)*. 4 Vols. Leipzig.

Simons, J., 1959. *The Geographical and Topographical Lists of the Old Testament*. Leiden.

Stern, M., 1974. *Greek and Latin Authors on Jews and Judaism* I. Jerusalem.

Stadelmann, R., 1967. *Syrisch-Palastnensische Gottheiten in Agypten*. Leiden.

Thompson, T.L., 1974. *The History of the Patriarchal Narratives*. Berlin.

Towers, J.K., 1959. The Red Sea. *JNES* 18:150-153.

Tresson, P., 1935-1938. in inscription de Chechenq Iet au Musée du Caire: une frappant example d'impôt progressif en matiriere religieuse. In *Mélange Maspero*. *MIFAO* 66, vol. I. Cairo. 1935-1938: 817-830.

Van Seters, J., 1975. *Abraham in History and Tradition*. New Haven.

Vandier, J., 1952. *Manuel d'Archeologie Egyptienne*. Paris.

————. 1965. Lousaas et (Hathor) Nebet-Hetepet II. Re'E 7: 89-176.

Ward, W.A., 1976. Some Personal Names of the Hyksos Period Rulers and Notes on the Epigraphy of their Scarabs. *UF* 8: 353-370.

Wiseman, J.D., 1956. *Chronicles of Chaldean Kings*. London: Trustees of the British Museum.

Wright, G.R.H., 1970. The Passage of the Sea. *Göttinger Miszellen* 3:55.

Yoyotte, J., 1961. Les Principautés du Delta. Pp. 121-181 of *Mélanges Maspero* I/4. Cairo.

8

Comments on the "Exodus"

Manfred Bietak

BEING an Egyptologist I feel somehow embarrassed to comment on problems surrounding the theme of "the Exodus". Such a topic discussed by generations of Old Testament scholars is highly delicate and the longer it is debated without increase of sources the more we have the stress of distinguishing ourselves by presenting the same facts in a new version. This implies the danger of distorting the original message by over-sophisticated exegesis. I therefore felt full sympathy with the frustration expressed by the speaker about this theme, particularly as it was presented with great scholarly skill, but I do not necessarily share Professor Redford's pessimism.

In order to facilitate our look at the objectives of Old Testament studies we may define these objectives in the following way:

1. The historical truth behind the story.

2. How the traditions transformed the historical events.

The first of the objectives can probably never be achieved, but there is some chance of approaching objective No. 1 indirectly by first exploring objective No. 2. But in order to present something new we need new sources and when they are not available from Old Testament documents, we have to try to integrate new sources from outside Old Testament studies. In the following, an example from our own studies (Fig. 1) will be presented, in order to illustrate how it may be possible to sort out and explain misleading traditions in order to isolate more likely possibilities.

After the Delta capital of the Ramessides, *Piramesse* (now generally located at Tell al-Dab 'a-Qantir) lost its function and was abandoned, its ruins served as a huge quarry furnishing the new important towns of the 21st and 22nd Dynasties with stone material. Particularly the temples of the two residences of the Bubastite kings in Tanis in the North and Bubastis in the South profited from this quarry (Habachi: in preparation; van Seters 1966:127-151). By the transportation of statues, stelae and other monuments, cultic representations of the gods of Ramesses (of Piramesse) were also transferred to the new places and to others as well. These gods can be considered as specific definitions of important divinities in connection with Ramesses II.

Several hundred years later, during the time of the 30th Dynasty, in the 4th century B.C., we suddenly have evidence about secondary cults for the gods of Ramesses in Tanis in the North and Bubastis in the South (Bietak 1975:219f.; *idem* 1981; *idem* 1982 IV:128-146). In Tanis we even have the specification of "Amun of Ramesses of Piramesse".

Those secondary cults surely were caused by the monuments coming originally from Piramesse and obviously in the 4th century B.C. people in Tanis believed, because of the many Ramesside monuments there, that the site of Tanis had been originally the famous Delta residence Piramesse in the remote past, while people in Bubastis at least held the opinion that the site of Piramesse was nearby.

This position not only logically, but also chronologically would explain the identification attempts of post-exilic Jewish scholars about the town of Ramesses and also the localisation of the route of the Exodus, again using Ramesses as a starting point (Ex. 12.37). They depended in their search for localisation on the Egyptian contemporary opinion.

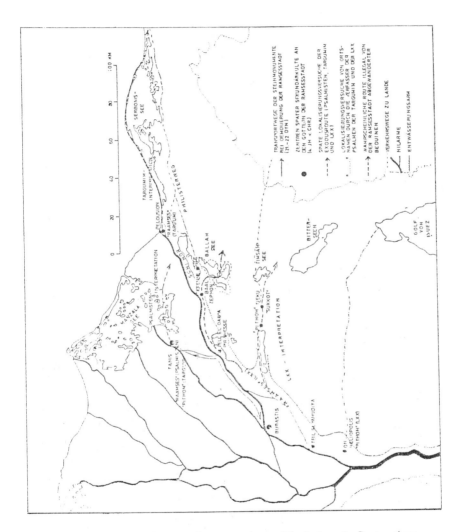

Fig. 1 — Geography of Exodus interpretations of Psalmists, the Septuaginta-compilers, of the Manethonian tradition and Targum interpretations according to modern geographical studies.

According to Psalm 78 which is of post-exilic date (Kuhlewein 1973:99), the site of Ramesses clearly is located at Tanis and also the "Sea of Reeds" in the "fields of Tanis" while the LXX sees the scenery of Ramesses in or near the Wadi Tumilat area, which is just east of Bubastis. Only in this way may we understand, why Joseph coming from the residence was meeting his father in Heroonpolis (in Wadi Tumilat) in the land of Ramesses (=Goshen) (LXX; Gen. 46.28-29).

A third version about the localisation of Ramesses, clearly meaning Avaris-Piramesse again, can be deducted from the third century B.C. onwards by the Manethonian tradition according to Flavius Josephus. He clearly brings this town in relationship to Pelusium (Contra Apionem I.26-33; 228-303). It seems to be a genuine version of Manetho as the same story about the lepers is also related to us in a very simplified version by Hekataios of Abdera in the 4th century B.C.

All these versions of the localisation of Ramesses and of the beginning of the route of the Exodus can be dismissed as the wrong traditions.[1] They only appear at the moment, when we have the secondary cults of the gods of Ramesses in Tanis and Bubastis and probably also in Pelusium. The origin and source of the monuments and cults of these gods was, however, the site of Piramesse, now definitely localized at Tell el-Dab 'a-Qantir.[2] This site is situated in the midst of those places which got a share of the monuments and glory of Piramesse — a very misleading situation for traditions and their interpretation. But once these stages of transportation of monuments, the creation of secondary cults and the secondary formation of opinions about the town of Piramesse become clear, the remaining options of Exodus localisation become very narrow, and here we really have a chance to start our approach to our first objective by finding the most likely circumstances for the event in historical and in geographical terms.

Let us start with the latter. When the town Ramesses is

identical with Piramesse then the geographical starting point of the event would have been Tell el-Dab'a-Qantir. In this case the route of departure is limited according to the clear reconstruction of water branches in antiquity. First of all one has to pass the narrow opening into the Nile Delta formed by the Pelusiac and the Bahr el-Baqar drainage system and one has to follow the Darb el-Sultan (Bietak 1975:135f.). Finally, in the environs of Defenne (Daphnai), which is a likely location for Ba'al Zephon (Aime '-Giron. 1940:433-436),[3] one comes to the decision either to pass the frontier at Sile (Zaru) or to evade it and pass through the Ballah lakes in order to reach wells east of that lake. This lake is a most likely location for the Yam Suph. An Egyptian homonym, the P'-Tjufy, is mentioned parallel with the Shi-Hor as a water boundary in connection with a hymn about Piramesse.[4] The most likely location of the Shi-Hor is the long narrow lake and water branch north of the Isthmus of Qantara, accompanying the Road of Horus, while the P'-Tjufy (Papyrus swamps), the Ballah lakes south of the Isthmus, are the most logical places. According to their situation they were inviting for Beduins either to enter or to leave Egypt illegally.

Unfortunately the mutual identification of Piramesse is not unchallenged, particularly by Donald Redford, because of the lack of the preceding *Pi* (i.e., *pr*) in the Old Testament (Redford 1963:407-418) and now we also have heard that the location of Pithom of the Old Testament is highly uncertain and its references in connection with the Exodus may have been caused by a very late tradition.

So objective No. 1, the historical truth, seems to be more remote than before. However, we should not relinquish our possibilities for this objective, when it is not cogently necessary. There is a chance at least to approach the historical truth when a series of circumstances have a logical connection to a tradition, particularly when we have succeeded in explaining wrong traditions.

First of all let me comment about the identifications of Ramesses and Pithom: A.H. Gardiner and, following him, W. Helck have already shown that also in ancient Egyptian versions the preceding Pi- of Piramesse can be omitted when *"p' dmj"* (i.e., "the town") is put afterwards (Gardiner 1918:137; Helck 1965:35-48). In such a way *R'-mssw-p'-dmj* could easily be transformed into another language in an abbreviated way as "Ramesses", especially as there always was the association with the king who gave the town his name.

Concerning the situation of the biblical Pithom, of course there had been several places with this name, but not many (Gauthier 1925-1931 II:59-61). This also led E. Uphill to locate it in Heliopolis (Uphill 1969:15-39). He followed an uncertainty which had already tempted the LXX-compilers, who allowed a gloss to Pithom, i.e., Heliopolis, to slip into the text as Pithom and Heliopolis (Ex. 1.11). But why should we try to explain a more complicated theory about Pithom when we do have a Pithom which would fit logically into the historical-geographical context? The most prominent Pithom was situated in the Wadi Tumilat. It is mentioned several times in connection with Tjeku (Gauthier 1925-1931 II: 59-61). Especially well known is the quotation in papyrus Anastasi VI (4.16) where a group of Edomites gained temporary permission to pass the boundary and advance up to the "lakes[5] of Pithom" in the name of Tjeku (i.e., Wadi Tumilat). This would fit well with the possible situation of the biblical Pithom which was obviously also within the reach of Beduins at the eastern edge of the Delta, after they had crossed the Sinai. The "lakes of Pithom" also fit well into the environment of the western half of the Wadi, which was filled originally with an overflow lake (Bietak 1975:88-90). The position of Pithom is also in accord with the situation of Patumos mentioned by Herodotus (II.158). It lay at the Red Sea channel which passed through the Wadi. From all sites in this region, only Tell el-Reṭâbeh has an occupation of the Ramesside period (contemporary with Ramesses-Piramesse) and this site is also situated at the eastern end of the lake in a dominant position regarding the Wadi. So we have a Pithom in the right place at the right time[6] in a parallel situation to the Ramesses-town, each blocking one of the two important entrances of the Eastern Delta. From this topographical and partly functional similarity we may understand the parallel quotation of Pithom and Ramesses in Exodus 1.11.

This is not just to defend an old and widely accepted opinion in connection with Pithom. New research material, based on geographical studies, strongly endorses and supplements this identification. Concerning the general situation for the sojourn to Egypt and the Exodus, I liked the approach of Professor Raphael Giveon who places the appearance of Proto-Israelites in the context of the Shosu Beduins. Prof. Giveon drew our attention to a fragmentary list of toponyms of Shosu Beduins including a toponym with the name Tʻ-sʻsw Yhw, which is not unlikely to be the earliest written record about a shrine of Yahweh (Giveon 1971:26f.). This could suggest that during the reign of Amenhotep III Beduins worshipping Yahweh appeared at the margin of Egyptian attention. This would fit fairly well into the other normally accepted fixed points such as the participation of Proto-Israelites in the building activity at Pithom and Ramesses and the Exodus, which must have happened sometime before the fifth regnal year of Merenptah.

Of course one may debate each of these points discussed in one way or the other with overly sophisticated arguments but it is the network of points which fits well together and which makes the whole context as defended and supplemented the most feasible background for the setting of the tradition.

Finally I would like to add another point which I was unable to render in the verbal version of the comments, because of time limits. If we accept the Exodus as a withdrawal of Proto-Israelites which met with obstacles on behalf of the Egyptians, then the geography of the Sinai would dictate the possibilities of the route. The northern route with the wells and cisterns of the Horus Road was well controlled by Egyptian garrisons and therefore impassable (Gardiner 1920: pl. XI). The middle route along the Mitla pass and Nakhl has too few wells to allow a larger body of people and animals to pass. So when the coastal road is closed, the only possibility to cross the Sinai is in the south along the Wadi Feiran region. The cluster of archaeological sites there (Rothenberg 1979: 112) and the fact that even the Romans had a systematically organized road there supports this impression. Of course the northern route also came into play by tradition, but the southern route is the logical one within the biblical context.

NOTES

1   Also the later Targum traditions insert Pelusium for Ramesses and Tanis for Pithom (Diez Macho, 1968 I: 314, 315, 481, 628; *idem*, 1970: 4, 5, 76, 77, 407, 440).
2   Habachi, 1954:501-559; v. Seters, 1966; Uphill, 1968:291-316; *idem* 1969:15-39; Bietak, 1982:128-146.
3   A Phoenician letter of the 6th century B.C. mentions Ba'al Zephon and the divinities worshipped in Daphnai.
4   Pap. Anastasi III, 2.11-12. Compare also the quotation in the Onomasticon of Amenope directly before Sile (Gardiner, 1947: Nr. 418-419).
5   *Birk(ab)ot*, more likely to be translated as "lakes" than as "pools".
6   Only in late tradition did Pithom become confused with Heroonpolis (cf. LXX Gen. 46.28-29 u. Bohairic version).

REFERENCES

Aime Giron, M., 1940. Ba'al Saphon et les dieux de Tahpanhes dans un nouveau Papyrus Phenicien. *ASAE* 40:433-460.
Bietak, M., 1975. *Tell el-Dab'a II*. Wien.
——— 1981. *Avaris and Piramesse*. London.
——— 1982. "Ramsesstaat" *Ld'A* V: p. 128-146.

Diez Macho., 1968. *Neophyti I.* Vol. I, Barcelona.

——— 1970. *Neophyty.* Vol. II, Madrid, Barcelona.

Gardiner, A.H., 1918. "The Delta Residence of the Ramessides" *JEA* 5:179-200.

Gardiner, A.H., and Litt P., 1940. "The Ancient Military Road Between Egypt and Palestine" *JEA* 6: pl. XI.

Gardiner, A.H., 1947. *Ancient Egyptian Onomastica.* Oxford, 418-419.

Gauthier, H., 1925-1931. *Dictionnaire des noms Geographiques Contenus dans les textes hierogliyphiques.* Cairo.

Giveon, R., 1971. *Les bedouins de Shosu de documents Egyptiens.* Leiden.

Habachi, L., 1954. Kanta'na-Quantir: Importance. *ASAE* 52:443-562.

——— *Tell el-Dab'a and Qantir.* Vol. I.

——— *Unters. Zweigstelle kairo des Ostreichischen Archaologischen Institus II.*

Helck, W., 1965. Ikw und die Ramses-stadt. *V.T.* 15:35-48.

Kuhlewein, J., 1973. *Geschichte des Psalmen, Calwer Theologische Monographien.* A2. Stuttgart: 99.

Redford, D.B., 1963. Exodus I11, VI 13:401-418.

Rothenberg, B., 1979. *Sinai*, Bern: 112.

Uphill, E., 1968. Pithom and Raamses: Their Location and Significance I. *JNES* 27:291-316.

——— 1969. Pithom and Raamses: Their Location and Significance II. *JNES* 28:15-39.

Van Seters, J., 1966. *The Hyksos — A New Investigation.* New Haven: 127-151.

THE CONTRIBUTORS

ITZHAQ BEIT-ARIEH
Principal Research Associate of Archaeology, Tel Aviv University.

MANFRED BIETAK
Prof. of Egyptology, University of Vienna and Director of the Ostrian Institute of Archaeology, Cairo.

TRUDE DOTHAN
Prof. of Archaeology, The Hebrew University.

RAPHAEL GIVEON (deceased)
Associate Prof. of Egyptian Archaeology, Tel Aviv University.

RAM GOPHNA
Associate Prof. of Archaeology, Tel Aviv University.

ELIEZER D. OREN
Prof. of Archaeology and Near Eastern History, Ben Gurion University of the Negev.

ANSON F. RAINEY
Prof. of Ancient Near Eastern Culture and Semitic Linguistics, Tel Aviv University,

DONALD B. REDFORD
Prof. of Egyptology, University of Toronto.